COULD THE RAPTURE HAPPEN TODAY?

MARK HITCHCOCK

Multnomah® Publishers *Sisters, Oregon*

COULD THE RAPTURE HAPPEN TODAY?
published by Multnomah Publishers, Inc.
© 2005 by Mark Hitchcock
International Standard Book Number: 1-59052-343-1

Cover design by Kirk DouPonce, DogEaredDesign.com
Cover image by jo Son/Getty Images
Interior design and typeset by Katherine Lloyd, The DESK

Unless otherwise indicated, Scripture quotations are from:
New American Standard Bible (NASB) © 1960, 1977, 1995
by the Lockman Foundation. Used by permission.
Other Scripture quotations are from:
Holy Bible, New Living Translation (NLT)
©1996. Used by permission of Tyndale House Publishers, Inc.
All rights reserved.
The Message © 1993 by Eugene H. Peterson
The Holy Bible, King James Version (KJV)

Multnomah is a trademark of Multnomah Publishers, Inc.,
and is registered in the U.S. Patent and Trademark Office.
The colophon is a trademark of Multnomah Publishers, Inc.
Printed in the United States of America

For information:
MULTNOMAH PUBLISHERS, INC.
601 N. LARCH ST. • SISTERS, OREGON 97759

Library of Congress Cataloging-in-Publication Data
Hitchcock, Mark.
Could the rapture happen today? / Mark Hitchcock
    p. cm.
ISBN 1-59052-343-1
1. Rapture (Eschatology) 2. Eschatology. 3. Second Advent. I. Title.
BT887.H56 2005
236'.9--dc22
                                                            2005011928

05 06 07 08 09 10—10 9 8 7 6 5 4 3 2 1 0

CONTENTS

INTRODUCTION

A few years ago I ran across one of those innumerable top-ten lists that seem to be making the rounds these days. This one was titled *The Top Ten Ways to Know If You Are Obsessed with Prophecy*. Seeing that I spend a fair amount of time researching and speaking on this subject, I thought I should take a closer look. Here's how it shapes up.

1. You always leave the top down on your convertible in case the Rapture happens.
2. You never buy green bananas.
3. You talk your church into adapting the sixties pop song "Up, Up, and Away" as a Christian hymn.
4. Barcode scanners make you nervous.
5. You refuse a tax refund check because the amount comes to $666.
6. You can name more signs of the times than you can commandments.
7. You believe that there is an original Greek and Hebrew text with Scofield's notes.
8. You believe that the phrase "church fathers" refers to Hal Lindsey and Tim LaHaye.
9. You get goose bumps when you hear a trumpet.
10. You use the Left Behind books as devotional reading.[1]

While I wouldn't say that I am *obsessed* with Bible prophecy, I am certainly very interested in it. More than any other single thing, studying the end times has helped me to understand the whole Bible. And while there are many truths about the end times that have deeply affected my life, one truth stands out above all others: the Rapture.

I will never forget the first time that I heard this great truth explained and how it captured my heart and imagination. The Rapture is more than an event. It's a *person*. It's all about Jesus coming personally from heaven to meet His saints in the air, taking us back to heaven with Him, and keeping us in His presence forever.

The force of this truth has never left me. I think about it almost every day. It has shaped my life…and it continues to do so.

Maybe you're asking, "Why *another* book about the Rapture?"

The pre-Tribulation Rapture view has been popularized in the last few years in the mega-selling Left Behind series by Tim LaHaye and Jerry Jenkins. But the popular acceptance of this view has brought out the critics in full force. The pre-Tribulation Rapture position is under attack more today than at any other time in history.

The purpose of this book is to look at what God's Word says about the Rapture and its timing in relation to the coming Tribulation period. I will defend the pre-Tribulation position— the only view that holds that the Rapture could happen today, at any moment, in the next blink of your eyes.

Most of the books that I've read on the Rapture are either too shallow or too scholarly, too in-depth for the average person or too skimpy on details. I don't profess to be able to hit the happy medium in the middle of the bull's-eye, but my goal is for this book to serve as a plain, clear, simple, thorough guide that explains the biblical teaching on the Rapture.

To guide us through this subject, I've divided the book into four basic parts.

1. The *Truth* of the Rapture (What is it?)
2. The *Timing* of the Rapture (When will it occur in relation to the Tribulation?)
3. *Questions* about the Rapture (ten questions commonly asked by people like you and me)
4. The *Teaching* of the Rapture for Today (how the truth of the Rapture should affect our daily lives)

I will have to make a few assumptions as we move forward together. I will assume that you, the reader, have at least a basic knowledge of a few key events that will take place in the end times. So, just to make sure that we're on the same page at the outset, let's do a brief review and define a few key terms that you will see sprinkled throughout the book.

The Rapture of the church to heaven

The Rapture is an event that could occur at any moment. In that split second, all who have personally trusted in Jesus Christ as their Savior—both the living and the dead—will be caught up to meet the Lord in the air. They will go with Him back up to heaven and return back to the earth with Him at least seven years later at His second coming (see John 14:1–3; 1 Corinthians 15:50–58; 1 Thessalonians 4:13–18).

The seven-year Tribulation period

The Tribulation is the final seven years of this age, beginning with a peace treaty between Israel and the Antichrist and ending with the second coming of Christ back to earth. During this time the Lord will pour out His wrath upon the earth in successive waves of judgment. But the Lord will also pour out His grace by saving millions of people during this time (see Revelation 6–19).

The three-and-a-half-year world empire of Antichrist

In this last half of the Tribulation, the Antichrist will rule the world politically, economically, and religiously. The entire world will give allegiance to him or suffer persecution and death (see Revelation 13:1–18).

The campaign of Armageddon

The campaign or war of Armageddon is the final event of the Great Tribulation when all the armies of the earth gather to come against Israel and attempt once and for all to eradicate the Jewish people (see Revelation 14:19–20; 16:12–16; 19:19–21).

The second coming of Christ to earth

The climactic event of human history is the literal, physical, visible, glorious return of Jesus Christ back to earth to destroy the armies of the world, which are gathered in Israel, and to set up His kingdom on earth.

The one-thousand-year reign of Christ on earth

After the glorious appearing of Christ, Satan will be bound and imprisoned in the abyss for 1,000 years (see Revelation 20:1–3). This one-thousand-year period is often called the Millennium. During this time Jesus will rule and reign over the restored earth. Believers who survive the Tribulation period will enter the millennial kingdom in human bodies. All other believers will rule and reign with Christ (see Revelation 19:4–6).

God's Blueprint for the End Times

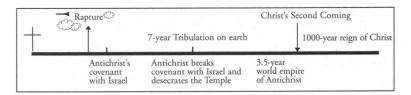

My sincere prayer is that God will use this book in your life to help you to discover the truth of the any-moment coming of Christ at the Rapture and to see that Jesus really could come today so that you will make sure that you are ready to meet the Lord when He appears. It could happen today!

Maranatha
Our Lord, come!
Mark Hitchcock

THE TRUTH
OF THE RAPTURE

When the subject of the Rapture comes up, it's natural that most people want to jump right to the "when" question. When will it happen? Which view is right? Will the Rapture take place before, in the middle of, or after the Great Tribulation?

But through the years I've found that many people don't really have a firm grasp of what the Rapture is. Most people still have a very fuzzy idea of what will really happen when the trumpet sounds. To make sure that we're all reading from the same playbook, I want to spend four chapters looking together at the truth of the Rapture.

Whether you are a relative novice in the area of Bible prophecy or an experienced veteran, I believe that these chapters will help you gain a clearer understanding of what this wondrous event is all about.

1

THE RAPTURE REVEALED

Current events in our world have focused attention like never before on the question of what the future holds for the world, the church, and Israel. In this explosive, ever-changing atmosphere it's only natural for people to wonder about the coming of Jesus Christ.

Will Jesus come?

When will Jesus come?

What will happen when He comes?

Most people, even those with little or no church background, seem to have a sense that this world is getting near its "closing time." There's an expectation that Jesus will come, possibly very soon, to rapture His people to heaven. Many people believe the Rapture to be the next event on God's prophetic calendar.

According to a *Newsweek* poll in May 2004, 55 percent of Americans "think that the faithful will be taken up to heaven in the Rapture."[2] That's incredible to me. Over half of the people in America believe in the event that has been commonly called "the Rapture."

I'm sure that many of the people who responded to this survey are somewhat unsure about the details of the Rapture. Others know something about it but hear about all the different views and get confused. For many more the whole idea is probably very vague and fuzzy.

So, to help cut through some of the confusion, I want to begin by considering the most basic question about the Rapture: *What is it?*

Simply stated, the rapture of the church is that future event when Jesus Christ will descend from heaven to resurrect the bodies of departed believers and to transform and translate the bodies of living believers immediately into His glorious presence in a moment of time and then escort them to heaven to live with Him forever.

That's it, in a nutshell.

The Rapture is the blessed hope of the church.

But if the Rapture is such a big deal, people often ask, why don't we find the word *rapture* in the Bible?

Why Isn't the Word *Rapture* in the Bible?

Several years ago a friend of mine and I were having lunch in a restaurant in downtown Oklahoma City. My friend had questions about the Bible and the end times, and the subject of the Rapture came up. What exactly would happen, he wanted to know, when the Rapture took place?

After I gave him a brief answer, a man from a nearby table came by our table as he was leaving. He said that he had overheard our conversation and wanted to let my friend know that what I had told him was all wrong. His main argument was that the word *rapture* doesn't even appear in the Bible. He asked how

I could believe in something that isn't even in the Bible.

He was right that the exact word *rapture* is missing from all the standard English translations of the Bible. But he was wrong to say that the event that we describe as the Rapture is not found in the Bible.

Here's why: If you were to read all 774,747 words in the King James Version of the Bible—or any other well-known translation, for that matter—you would find that the rude man in the restaurant was right. The word *rapture* simply isn't there. However, you would also look in vain for the words *Trinity*, *Bible*, or *grandfather* (in most translations). And yet we know that all of these things are very real and true.

The term *rapture* is taken from 1 Thessalonians 4:17: "Then we who are alive and remain will be *caught up* together with them in the clouds to meet the Lord in the air, and so we shall always be with the Lord" (italics added). In this verse, the words *caught up* are translated from the Greek word *harpazo*, which means "to snatch, seize, or take suddenly or vehemently."

The word *harpazo* appears thirteen times in the New Testament (see Matthew 11:12; 13:19; John 6:15; 10:12, 28–29; Acts 8:39; 23:10; 2 Corinthians 12:2, 4; 1 Thessalonians 4:17; Jude 1:23; Revelation 12:5). Take a moment to look up these verses and you will see that the word *harpazo* is variously translated as "take forcibly," "snatch," or "caught up."

Our English word *rapture*, as with so many English terms, derives from the Latin. Here's how it happened: In the fourth century AD, the great scholar Jerome translated the New Testament from the original Greek language to Latin. His translation is known as the Vulgate. In 1 Thessalonians 4:17, Jerome rendered the Greek word *harpazo* into Latin with the word *raep-*

tius. The Latin word *rapio* means "to seize, snatch, or seize away." This was eventually brought over to English as *rapture.*

So while it is true that the word *rapture* does not occur in most English translations of the Bible, the concept or doctrine of a catching away of living believers to meet the Lord is clearly stated in 1 Corinthians 15:51–55 and 1 Thessalonians 4:17. This doctrine could just as well be called the "catching away of the church," "the snatching away of the church," the "translation of the church," or the "*harpazo* of the church." But since the phrase "rapture of the church" is an excellent description of this event and has become the most common, accepted title for this event, there is no reason to change the terminology.

Don't let anyone lead you astray. The Rapture *is* in the Bible. But don't just take my word for it. See it for yourself in the pages of the Word of God.

Key Rapture Passages

While New Testament writers refer to the Rapture many times in the pages of the New Testament, three main passages provide the most detail. Carefully reading each of these passages will help you get a basic overview of the Rapture directly from Scripture.

Do not let your heart be troubled; believe in God, believe also in Me. In My Father's house are many dwelling places; if it were not so, I would have told you; for I go to prepare a place for you. If I go and prepare a place for you, I will come again and receive you to Myself, that where I am, there you may be also. (John 14:1–3)

Now I say this, brethren, that flesh and blood cannot inherit the kingdom of God; nor does the perishable inherit the imperishable. Behold, I tell you a mystery; we will not all sleep, but we will all be changed, in a moment, in the twinkling of an eye, at the last trumpet; for the trumpet will sound, and the dead will be raised imperishable, and we will be changed. For this perishable must put on the imperishable, and this mortal must put on immortality. But when this perishable will have put on the imperishable, and this mortal will have put on immortality, then will come about the saying that is written, "Death is swallowed up in victory. O death, where is your victory? O death, where is your sting?" The sting of death is sin, and the power of sin is the law; but thanks be to God, who gives us the victory through our Lord Jesus Christ. (1 Corinthians 15:50–57)

But we do not want you to be uninformed, brethren, about those who are asleep, so that you will not grieve as do the rest who have no hope. For if we believe that Jesus died and rose again, even so God will bring with Him those who have fallen asleep in Jesus. For this we say to you by the word of the Lord, that we who are alive and remain until the coming of the Lord, will not precede those who have fallen asleep. For the Lord Himself will descend from heaven with a shout, with the voice of the archangel and with the trumpet of God, and the dead in Christ will rise first. Then we who are alive and remain will be caught up together with them in the clouds to meet the Lord in the air, and so we shall always be with the Lord. Therefore comfort one another with these words. (1 Thessalonians 4:13–18)

Now that you have a basic idea of the truth of the Rapture, let's get into a little more detail.

THE 10 *R*'S
OF THE RAPTURE

By far the clearest, most detailed description of the Rapture is found in 1 Thessalonians 4:13–18. The apostle Paul included ten key points or aspects of the Rapture when he penned this passage. I like to call them the "10 *R*'s of the Rapture."

While I will use 1 Thessalonians 4:13–18 as the primary text for this section, I will also bring in parts of John 14:1–3 and 1 Corinthians 15:50–57 to clarify and reinforce the great truths from 1 Thessalonians.

1. The Reason (1 Thessalonians 4:13)

> But we do not want you to be uninformed, brethren, about those who are asleep, so that you will not grieve as do the rest who have no hope.

Why did Paul present this teaching on the Rapture to this particular audience at this time?

He gives the reason himself, saying that he wrote this passage to eliminate ignorance among those brothers and sisters—to inform them of the truth. Paul wasn't like many today who say, "We don't need to know about Bible prophecy." On the contrary, the Apostle declares, "I don't want you to be uninformed about the Rapture and the end times."

Playing off of the King James rendering of this passage ("I would not have you to be ignorant, brethren"), Warren Wiersbe once said that the fastest-growing church in America is the church of the ignorant brethren. Paul wrote to correct this problem.

Paul wrote the letter of 1 Thessalonians from the Greek city of Corinth in about AD 50, during his second missionary journey. Paul came to Europe after receiving the Macedonian vision in Acts 16. Paul, Luke, Timothy, and Silas landed at Neapolis and then made their way ten miles down the road to the city of Philippi. After being run out of town (nothing new for these guys), their next stop was the city of Thessalonica. Paul stayed in the city for at least three weeks—and possibly for as long as a few months (see Acts 17:1–2).[3] During that stay, a church was born.

While among the Thessalonians, Paul evidently taught extensively about end-time events, including the Rapture, the Second Coming, and the final world ruler or Antichrist. (How would you have liked to attend *that* prophecy seminar?)

Before long, however, the familiar pattern repeated itself, and the Jewish leaders and city fathers ran the Apostle out of town, and he hit the road for Berea. From there he moved to Athens and finally to Corinth, where he resided for eighteen months (see Acts 18:11).

While in Corinth Paul received news from Timothy that the

fledgling church at Thessalonica was growing and standing strong. But Timothy also brought news about a serious concern among the believers there. In the few months since Paul's departure, a few of their number had died. This caused the Thessalonians to wonder what would happen to their deceased loved ones in Christ. Would they miss the Rapture that Paul had told them about? Would they be left out? Would they be second-class citizens when the Rapture occurred? Would they miss out on the spiritual blessings that those who were alive would receive when the Lord came? How would they fit into God's future program?

Paul wrote 1 Thessalonians 4:13-18 to clarify his previous oral teaching on the Rapture and to assure the confused and distressed Thessalonians that not only would the dead in Christ not miss out on the Rapture, but that they would "rise first" (v. 16) when Christ came for His church.

2. The Root (1 Thessalonians 4:14a)

For if we believe that Jesus died and rose again…

Our belief in the death and resurrection of Jesus Christ forms the root, the foundation, the core of our teaching on the Rapture. Our Lord's death on the cross, where He paid the price for our sins with His precious blood, secured our place in heaven. Because Jesus rose from the dead, we have assurance that God accepted the death of Christ on our behalf. This is the very bedrock of our Christian faith. Because He died for us, we are forgiven. Because He was raised, we too will be raised.

The Bible calls Christ's resurrection the "first fruits," the guarantee, the blueprint for the resurrection of His people (see 1 Corinthians 15:20). He is the Head of the body, and we are the members of that body. For that reason, what happens to the Head must happen to the members of the body. His victory over death and the grave assures our victory

The root of the Rapture is Christ's death and resurrection.

3. The Rejoining (1 Thessalonians 4:14b)

Even so God will bring with Him those who have fallen asleep in Jesus.

A natural question that the Thessalonians would have asked (and you and I might ask it as well) is "How are those who have died in Christ rejoined to their bodies?" The answer? By resurrection.

At the Rapture God will bring the perfected spirits of believers back with Him from heaven. Those perfected spirits will be rejoined with their glorified bodies, which will be raised.

To properly grasp this idea of rejoining at the Rapture, it's important that we understand what occurs at the moment of physical death. Death in the Bible always means *separation*, never annihilation or cessation of existence.

In the Garden of Eden God told Adam that the day he ate of the fruit of the tree of the knowledge of good and evil, he would surely die (see Genesis 2:17). When Adam and Eve ate of the fruit they did not die physically. They *began* to die physically. Adam died 930 years later. But in the very moment that they ate the fruit they died spiritually, just as God had said. Separated and alienated from their Creator, Adam and Eve sensed their guilt and shame and made garments out of leaves to cover their naked bodies and hide their sin.

A person who is *spiritually* dead is a person who is spiritually separated from God (see Ephesians 2:1). Likewise, when a person dies *physically* he or she does not cease to exist. There is a separation between the material part (the body) and immaterial part (the soul/spirit) of the person. When this separation occurs the body "falls asleep" and is buried. But the soul/spirit, the immaterial part of the person, goes immediately to heaven if the person is a believer (see 2 Corinthians 5:8; Philippians 1:23). During the time between a person's death and resurrection the person lives in a disembodied state that Paul refers to as being "naked" in 2 Corinthians 5:3.

Notice that in 1 Thessalonians 4:13–15 the words *fallen asleep* or *asleep* occur three times. It's a common Biblical euphemism for death (see Matthew 27:52; John 11:11; Acts 7:60; 13:36). This is not referring to the idea of soul sleep that is taught by Seventh Day Adventists and Jehovah's Witnesses. The doctrine of soul sleep maintains that when a person dies the soul, as well as the body, sleeps in the grave, unconscious until the resurrection. In other words, the body returns to dust while the soul becomes unconscious.

The Bible, however, clearly teaches that when a believer dies his or her soul goes immediately into the conscious presence of the Lord. Many Bible passages support this idea: Luke 16:19–31; 23:39–43; Acts 7:56–60; 2 Corinthians 5:8; Philippians 1:23.

The "sleep" in 1 Thessalonians 4:13–15 refers to the sleep of the body, not the soul. The Greek word used here for "fall asleep" is the word *koimao*. It was used in ancient times to refer to the place where dead bodies were buried. These places came to be known as *koimeteria*. We get our English word *cemetery* from this word. The word *koimao* was also used in ancient times to refer to dormitories or sleeping places. A cemetery is a "dormitory" for the sleeping bodies of those who have died.

I read somewhere about the inscription on a gravestone in

England for a man named Solomon Peas. Here are the words that were carved into the granite:

Here lies the body of Solomon Peas

Under the grass and under the trees

But Peas is not here only the pod

Peas shelled out and went to God

This epitaph graphically expresses the truth of physical death for a Christian. The "peas" shell out and go to God, while the "pod" remains and is buried. A separation occurs.

At the time of the Rapture the immaterial and material will be rejoined. The separation that occurred at physical death will be forever reversed. The Lord will bring the perfected spirit of each believer from heaven, and the body of each believer will be raised up incorruptible to meet his or her spirit in the air and be rejoined forever.

The Rapture will be a glorious rejoining.

4. The Revelation (1 Thessalonians 4:15a)

For this we say to you by the word of the Lord...

The next question that someone might ask is, "Paul, how do you know about all this? What's your source of information?"

Paul's answer is that he got it directly from the Lord: "By the word of the Lord" (v. 15).

Paul probably received this from the Lord during one of Christ's personal appearances to him—or perhaps during his time of training in Arabia (see Galatians 1:17). Regardless of when he received it, Paul wants there to be no mistake. What he records in this passage is divinely revealed. It's not something that he made up on his own.

You can count on it!

5. The Reappearing
(1 Thessalonians 4:15b–16)

…that we who are alive and remain until the coming of the Lord, will not precede those who have fallen asleep. For the Lord Himself will descend from heaven with a shout, with the voice of the archangel and with the trumpet of God.

At the end of verse 15 the Apostle begins to lay out the sequence of events that will occur at the time of the Rapture. He explains that we who are alive at the time of the Rapture will not precede or go before those who have died. In the Greek there's a strong double negative (*ou me*) that means "by no means" or "not at all." In this passage that double negative emphatically expresses the fact that those who are alive will by no means precede those who have died. No way!

At the time of the Rapture the first thing that will occur is that the Lord Himself will come again in the clouds: "The Lord Himself will descend from heaven" (v. 16). Jesus won't send an angel or some representative. The Lord Himself will come! The Rapture will open with the personal reappearance of Jesus in the sky.

The Shout

Jesus will return accompanied by three things. First, there will be a commanding shout from the lips of Jesus Himself. Jesus spoke of this shout in John 5:28: "Do not marvel at this; for an hour is coming, in which all who are in the tombs will hear His voice."

The Greek word translated "shout" was used in ancient times to refer to a general shouting to his troops, a driver shouting to push his horses to greater speed, a hunter spurring on his dogs in pursuit of prey, and a captain of rowers encouraging them to row more vigorously.[4]

This commanding shout is the last of three great cries or commands of the Savior:

1. The cry from the *cemetery* when Lazarus was raised (see John 11:43–44). Someone has aptly pointed out that Jesus specifically said, "Lazarus come forth" (v. 43) because if He had just said, "Come forth," all the dead bodies would have come out of the tombs.
2. The cry from the *cross* when the dead came to life (see Matthew 27:50–53).
3. The cry from the *clouds* that will come when the dead in Christ are raised at His coming (see 1 Thessalonians 4:16).

Notice how at each of these cries the dead are resurrected.

The Summons

Second, there will be the call of the archangel—almost certainly Michael the archangel (see Jude 1:9). Michael's call may be to summon the other angels for this great meeting in the sky. Or, it may be a cry of victory and rejoicing. The Rapture will be great victory for believers, but also for the angels when the Lord comes for His church. It will be a tremendous victory over the forces of evil.

The Trumpet

Third, the trumpet of God will sound. Trumpets in Scripture are often used to signal an assembling together or a marching forward. This trumpet will sound to announce the Lord's arrival and to summon His people to meet Him in the air. In 1 Corinthians 15:52, a parallel passage to 1 Thessalonians 4:16, Paul refers to this trumpet as the "last trumpet."

This reference to the "last trumpet" has caused a great deal of misunderstanding.[5] Mid-Tribulationists often try to link this trumpet to the seventh trumpet in Revelation 11. They equate the seventh trumpet in Revelation 11:15–17 with the "last trumpet" in 1 Corinthians 15:52 and the trumpet in 1 Thessalonians 4:16. This identification is probably the key point to the mid-Tribulationist view.

A close examination of the two passages, however, reveals that these trumpets should not be equated with each other. All that they really have in common is that they are both trumpets. Note the stark differences between the trumpets in these two contexts.

	Trumpet in 1 Thessalonians 4 and 1 Corinthians 15:52	Trumpet in Revelation 11
Subject	Church	Wicked World
Result	Catching up of the church to be with the Lord	Judgment of the godless world
Character	Trumpet of God's grace	Trumpet of God's judgment
Timing	Signals the close of the life of the church on earth. It's the last trumpet of the church age.	Marks a climax in the progression of tribulation judgments.

Post-Tribulationists, on the other hand, often equate the last trumpet in 1 Thessalonians 4 and 1 Corinthians 15 with the trumpet in Matthew 24:31, which appears at the end of the Tribulation: "And He will send forth His angels with a great trumpet and they will gather together His elect from the four winds, from one end of the sky to the other." Post-Tribulationists contend that since the trumpet in Matthew 24:31 is at the end of the Tribulation and is therefore the last trumpet, it must be the same as the last trumpet in 1 Corinthians 15:52

Not so! The only similarity between these trumpets is that both are used to gather the Lord's people. Again, as this comparison reveals, the differences are marked.

	Trumpet in 1 Thessalonians 4 and 1 Corinthians 15	Trumpet in Matthew 24:31
Subject	Church	Jewish believers in the Great Tribulation
Circumstances	Connected with the raising of believers who have died	No mention of resurrection. Focus is on regathering living believers who have been scattered over the earth.
Result	Uniting of the raised dead with the living dead in a great meeting with the Lord in the air	The elect are living believers who are regathered from all over the earth to meet the Lord, who has returned to the earth in an open display of glory.
Signs	Preceded by no signs	Preceded by many signs

Simply because the trumpet in 1 Corinthians 15 is called the "last" trumpet does not mean that it is the last trumpet in God's whole prophetic program. The last trumpet that will sound in conjunction with the Rapture is the final trumpet of this age. It's the last trumpet of the church age. It's not the last trumpet that will ever sound.

Dr. John Walvoord provides an excellent illustration that clarifies this issue:

> At Dallas Theological Seminary there are classes regulated by a system of bells. These bells ring several times each hour. The question sometimes arises concerning what bell has been ringing. There is a series of bells: a three-minute warning bell, then the bell to start the class, another warning bell five minutes before the end of the class, and finally the last bell closing the class period. When the warning bell preceding the beginning of the class rings, someone might ask, "Is that the last bell?" The answer would be, "No, that is the first bell." A few minutes later the last bell—which is the bell that begins the class—would ring. After forty-five minutes, the warning bell near the end of the class session would ring. Someone then might ask, "Is that the first bell?" The reply of course would be, "Yes, that is the first bell." In another five minutes, the bell would ring again—the last bell for the class hour. In a few minutes the whole cycle of bells begins again for the next hour. The last bell for one class hour would ring before the first bell of the next hour. How ridiculous it would be to make all the "last bells" one and the same. So it is with the trumpets of Scripture. The last trumpet for the church is long before any of the trumpets of Revelation.[6]

The last trumpet of the Rapture is the final trumpet of this age that will summon God's people to the great meeting in the sky.

The Sights and Sounds

As I read this incredible account of what will happen someday with the shout, the voice, and the blast of the trumpet, another question comes to mind: Will those who are left behind on earth at the Rapture be able to hear the sound of the trumpet, the commanding shout of Christ, and the call of the archangel?

While I wouldn't be hard and fast on this, it seems to me that the unbelieving world *will* hear these sounds—but they won't see anything. I draw support for this view from Acts 9:1–7, with the story of the conversion of Saul of Tarsus on the road to Damascus.

In that life-changing encounter, Saul saw a great light from heaven that flashed around him, and he heard a thundering voice from heaven. But Acts 9:7 says, "The men who traveled with him stood speechless, hearing the voice but seeing no one." We see the same thing in John 12:28–30, where the voice of God thundered from heaven and the people present heard the sound but couldn't understand what was said. Also, in Daniel 10:7, when Daniel received a great vision the men who were with him didn't see the vision but were filled with terror. "Now I, Daniel, alone saw the vision, while the men who were with me did not see the vision; nevertheless, a great dread fell on them, and they ran away to hide themselves."

It may be the same way at the Rapture. The unbelievers left behind may hear the sounds and the voices but not see a thing. Opponents of the pre-Tribulation view often call it the "secret Rapture" view.

Secret? I don't think so! Something so spectacular and global in scope won't be a secret. The great sounds will reverberate around the globe, adding to the confusion, chaos, terror, dread, and fear that the world will experience when the Lord calls His people home.

The Speed

How long will it take for all the separate events of the Rapture to take place? According to the Bible the entire event will happen instantaneously. First Corinthians 15:52 says that these things will take place "in a moment, in the twinkling of an eye." The word for "moment" is the Greek word *atomos*, from which we get our English word *atom*. It refers to that which cannot be divided.

At the time that Paul wrote these words no one could conceive of splitting the atom. *Atomos* to the Greeks simply meant the smallest particle of matter. Today we would translate this phrase as "in an atomic second," "in a split second," or "in a flash."

And how about "in the twinkling of an eye"? The Greek word for "twinkling" is *rhipe*. This word has been interpreted two ways. First, some believe that it refers to the incalculably fast flash of time that it takes for light to reflect—"twinkle" or gleam—off of the human eye. I don't know how long that takes, but it's very quick. It reminds me of a coach I heard one time describing how fast a certain player was. The proud coach said that his player was so fast that he could turn off the light in his room at night and be in bed before it got dark. That's fast.

Second, others believe that it refers to the time that it takes to blink your eye—"at the blink of an eye." Because this is the fastest movement in the human body, it's an excellent, universally understood expression to indicate the speed at which something happens. I believe that this is probably the idea expressed in 1 Corinthians 15:52.

I read one time that it takes one-fiftieth of a second to blink your eye. The average person blinks twenty-five times a minute. (That means that during a ten-hour trip in a car going fifty-five mph, you drive thirty-three miles with your eyes closed!)

But regardless of which view you take of "in the twinkling of an eye," the point is crystal clear: All of this will happen in a flash. In a split second. It will be so fast that it will be unobservable to the human eye.

However, in order to help us better understand and grasp it, the Lord slows down the film in 1 Thessalonians 4:16–18 so that we can see it unfold frame by frame.

Let's move on to the next fame.

6. The Resurrection
(1 Thessalonians 4:15b–16)

...And the dead in Christ will rise first.

During the Civil War a group of soldiers had to spend a winter night without tents in an open field. During the night it snowed several inches, and at dawn the chaplain reported a strange sight. The snow-covered soldiers looked like the mounds of new graves, and when the bugle sounded reveille a man immediately rose from each mound of snow, dramatically reminding the chaplain of the coming resurrection of the dead.[7]

When Christ comes down from heaven, the first thing that will happen is that the bodies of deceased believers will be raised or resurrected and reunited to their perfected spirits, which have returned with the Lord. The dead in Christ will rise first. Someone has pointed out that the dead in Christ will rise first because they have six feet further to go. This might be true, but Paul is primarily showing the Thessalonians that their deceased loved ones won't be at any disadvantage. They not only won't miss the Rapture or any of its blessings, but they will actually get a head start on the living.

These resurrected bodies will be glorified, incorruptible bodies fit for the heavenly realm (see 2 Corinthians 5:1–5). Let's face it. As our outer man begins to fall apart, we begin to groan for glory. We eagerly anticipate our new, remodeled, perfect bodies in heaven. As 2 Corinthians 5:1–2 says,

> For we know that if the earthly tent which is our house is torn down, we have a building from God, a house not made with hands, eternal in the heavens. For indeed in this house we groan, longing to be clothed with our dwelling from heaven.

But when we begin to think about our future resurrection bodies we often have more questions than answers. While the Bible doesn't satisfy our curiosity about every detail, it does give us a basic idea of what our new, glorified bodies will be like.

Generally, we know from Scripture that our new bodies will be like the resurrected, glorified body of Jesus:

> For our citizenship is in heaven, from which also we eagerly wait for a Savior, the Lord Jesus Christ; who will transform the body of our humble state into conformity with the body of His glory, by the exertion of the power that He has even to subject all things to Himself. (Philippians 3:20–21)

> Beloved, now we are children of God, and it has not appeared as yet what we will be. We know that when He appears, we will be like Him, because we will see Him just as He is. (1 John 3:2)

What was Christ's resurrection body like?

- It consisted of flesh and bone (see Luke 24:39–40).
- He ate food (see Luke 24:41–43; John 21:12–15).
- He was recognized by His disciples (see Luke 24:31).
- He was not subject to normal laws of time and space. On two separate occasions, Jesus came right through the walls of the room where the disciples were meeting (see Luke 24:36; John 20:19, 26). On another occasion He vanished from sight (see Luke 24:31).

More specifically, the Bible gives several key facts about our future bodies in 1 Corinthians 15:35, 42–49:

But someone will say, "How are the dead raised? And with what kind of body do they come?"…So also is the resurrection of the dead. It is sown a perishable body, it is raised an imperishable body; it is sown in dishonor, it is raised in glory; it is sown in weakness, it is raised in power; it is sown a natural body, it is raised a spiritual body. If there is a natural body, there also a spiritual body. So also it is written, "The first man, Adam, became a living soul." The last Adam became a life-giving spirit. However, the spiritual is not first, but the natural; then the spiritual. The first man is from the earth, earthy; the second man is from heaven. As is the earthy, so also are those who are earthy; and as is the heavenly, so also are those who are heavenly. Just as we have borne the image of the earthy, we will also bear the image of the heavenly.

Eight Fabulous Facts About Our Future Bodies

1. They will never be subject to disease, decay, or death. They will be imperishable. Our present bodies are born with an expiration date. Our future bodies will never wear out.

2. They will be perfectly suitable to our new environment. They will be "heavenly" bodies.

3. They will each be unique and diverse from one another. Just as different stars and planets are unique and have varying degrees of glory, we will each maintain a uniqueness and diversity in heaven.

4. They will be vastly superior to our present bodies, as superior as mighty celestial bodies are from this small planet of ours.

5. They will be glorious—"full of glory." They will never disappoint us.

6. They will be powerful. The future body will be an invincible fortress. It will never get tired, never wear out, and never yield to sin.

7. They will be spiritual. This doesn't mean that they won't be real or physical. It simply means that our new bodies will allow us to fully express our spiritual nature.

8. They will have continuity with our present bodies yet will be vastly changed. In 1 Corinthians 15 Paul used the picture of planting a seed to represent the placing of a body in the ground at death (vv. 42–44). When you plant a seed in the ground there is continuity between what you put in the ground and what comes up. A barley seed produces barley. An acorn becomes an oak tree. A grain of wheat produces wheat. But

there is also vast change. Think of the difference between an acorn and a mighty oak. Or the difference between a brown, ugly, hairy tulip bulb and the beautiful flower. You can't imagine the grandeur and majesty of a mighty oak by looking at an acorn. That's the way it will be with our new bodies. There is continuity between the body (seed) that is buried (planted) but also incredible transformation that we can't imagine by looking at our earthly bodies.

Will the Graves Burst Open?

There's one more thing that I've always wondered about concerning this resurrection at the Rapture—and maybe you've thought about it too. Will the graves of believers all over the world be opened when the bodies are caught up to meet the Lord in the air? Of course, the tombs won't have to be opened to let the bodies out. The spiritual bodies could pass right through the ground without disturbing it at all.

But based on Matthew 27:52–53 it seems very likely to me that the graves of believers will be opened at the Rapture: "The tombs were opened, and many bodies of the saints who had fallen asleep were raised; and coming up out of the tombs after His resurrection they entered the holy city and appeared to many."

According to this verse, when Jesus died on the cross some of the tombs in Jerusalem were opened, and then after His resurrection on the third day deceased believers came forth from them to walk around the city. These resurrected believers were a kind of preview of the great resurrection at the Rapture. Since the tombs were opened back then, it seems logical to me that the same thing will occur at the Rapture. Also, remember that the tomb of Jesus was opened at His resurrection, not to let Him out, but to allow the disciples in to see that He was risen. It may be the same at the Rapture.

Think about the horror that this will cause on earth. There will be empty, opened tombs and graves all over the world. It will be the ultimate day of the living dead.

7. The Removal (1 Thessalonians 4:17a)

Then we who are alive and remain will be caught up.

We've spoken about the resurrection of the dead at the Rapture. But what about those who are still alive in that moment? There will be many living believers on earth when this event occurs. What will happen to them? Will they have to die first so they can be raised?

Not resurrection, but Rapture.

When the dead have been raised, living believers will immediately be transformed and translated into the presence of the calling Christ without ever tasting physical death. They will not sleep. They will be snatched up from the earth to meet Christ in the air. As we discussed on page 16, the words *caught up* are the English translation of the Greek word *harpazo*, which means "to seize or snatch."

Several years ago in the *B.C.* comic strip, father and son ants were sitting on top of an anthill. The boy ant was reading a joke book and said, "Here's a good one, Dad. What did one atheist say to another during the 'rapture of the church?'" The dad ant responded, "I don't know—what?" The son said, "I *told* you there was a catch to this."

There is a "catch" to the Rapture. All living believers will be "caught up" to be with the Lord without dying.

The World's Greatest Mystery

As 1 Corinthians 15:51 says, "We will not all sleep, but we will all be changed." This verse is often mounted on the door of church nurseries. It's certainly true of many children in a church nursery, but thanks be to God that it also will be true of millions of His children when the Savior descends from heaven. Millions of believers will never face the sting of death but will be removed or raptured directly into the presence of the Lord in the clouds. This is the mystery of the Rapture: the fact that millions of believers will do an end run on the grave, robbing the grim reaper of millions of victims.

In 1 Corinthians 15:51, we read these words: "Behold, I tell you a mystery; we will not all sleep, but we will all be changed." Why is the Rapture called a mystery?

A mystery in the New Testament is not some difficult puzzle to solve or unravel. It's not even something that's hard to figure out. A mystery is a truth that has never been revealed up to the time when it's unveiled and that man could never figure out on his own apart from divine revelation. Ephesians 3:5 defines a mystery as that "which in other generations was not made known to the sons of men, as it has now been revealed to His holy apostles and prophets in the Spirit." Verse 9 of the same chapter adds that a mystery is that "which for ages has been hidden in God who created all things." Colossians 1:26 further defines a New Testament mystery: "the mystery which has been hidden from the past ages and generations; but now has been manifested to His saints."

The fact that believers would be caught up to heaven without dying was a brand-new truth that had been hidden in God up to that time. It was a mystery—a totally new truth that had never been disclosed by God until 1 Corinthians 15. Actually, 1 Thessalonians was written by Paul before 1 Corinthians, but if you were reading the Bible straight through you would come to 1 Corinthians first. And if you read in your Bible straight through from Genesis 1 to 1 Corinthians 14, you would correctly conclude that the only way to get to heaven in your glorified body would be to die.

This reminds me of a story of a Sunday school teacher whose assignment was to explain to the six-year-olds in his class what someone had to do in order to go to heaven. In an attempt to discover what the kids already believed about the subject, he asked a few questions.

"If I sold my house and my car, had a big garage sale, and gave all my money to the church, would *that* get me into heaven?"

"NO!" the children all answered.

"If I cleaned the church every day, mowed the yard, and kept everything neat and tidy, would *that* get me into heaven?"

Again the answer was, "NO!"

"Well, then," he said, "if I was kind to animals and gave candy to all the children and loved my wife, would that get me into heaven?"

Again they all shouted, "NO!"

"Well, then, how *can* I get into heaven?"

A boy in the back row stood up and shouted, "YOU GOTTA BE DEAD!"[8]

Up until the time of Paul this answer was absolutely correct. But in 1 Corinthians 15 that all changed. The Lord unveiled through Paul the glorious mystery that a whole generation of believers will be transformed without tasting the sting of physical death. Millions of believers will be transformed into their new, glorified bodies in the amount of time that it takes to blink one's eye.

This is the glorious mystery of the Rapture. May we be the generation to experience this breathtaking event!

Picturing the Rapture

To help us picture what will happen to living believers at the Rapture, imagine that you have an old box in the attic that contains some nails that you want to use. But since the box has been in the attic for a long time, it's also filled with dust and sticks. The quickest way to retrieve the nails and leave the other stuff behind would be to hold a powerful magnet over the box. All of the objects in the box with the same properties as the magnet would be immediately attracted to it. The others would be left behind.

It will be the same way when the Lord comes for His church. Jesus will appear in the sky, and everyone who has His life will be attracted and drawn up to Him. All who are "in Christ" will be caught up. Those who have no part with Him, who don't share His properties, will be left behind.

It's critical that we understand that Jesus is not coming for good people, for people who attend church regularly, or for people who have undergone some particular rite or ritual. He's coming for those who are "in Him" by trusting Him and personally accepting Him as their Savior from sin. If you have never accepted Him, why not do it right now? Then you can be certain that you will be part of this great "snatching up."

8. The Reunion (1 Thessalonians 4:17)

...together with them in the clouds to meet the Lord in the air...

The dead in Christ and the living saints will all be raptured together and will meet the Lord in the air. We will see Jesus face to face for the very first time.

The old song "Face to Face" expresses this thought beautifully:

> *Face to face with Christ my Savior,*
> *face to face what will it be*
> *When with rapture I behold Him,*
> *Jesus Christ who died for me.*
> *Face to face, O blissful moment, face to face*
> *to see and know,*
> *Face to face with my Redeemer,*
> *Jesus Christ who loves me so.*

We will meet Jesus, and we will also be reunited with all our departed loved ones and friends who know the Lord.

This raises a very frequently asked question: will we know each other in heaven? Will we know and remember our loved ones and friends in heaven?

Almost every person has probably asked this question at one time or another. We want to know if we will recognize our friends and loved ones in heaven, and if they will know us. Interestingly, in a recent survey less than 50 percent of the respondents believed that they would see their friends, relatives, or spouses in heaven.

Well, I've got good news for you: we will not only see our friends and loved ones in heaven, but we will know them. In fact, we won't really know each other *until* we get to heaven. Only in heaven, when all the masks and facades are torn away, will we really know one another and enjoy intimate, unhindered fellowship.

The main passage that reveals that we will recognize each other in heaven is Luke 16:19–31. Remember how in that parable the rich man recognizes Lazarus in heaven and remembers all the facts about their relationship on earth. The rich man even remembers his five brothers who are still on earth.

For that matter, Scripture hints that we will even recognize people we *never* met here on earth! At the transfiguration of Jesus, Peter knew that the two men with Jesus were Elijah and Moses (see Matthew 17:1–4). Obviously, Peter had never met Moses and Elijah. How did he know who they were? It appears that he had an intuitive knowledge that enabled him to know immediately who they were. I believe that it will be the same way in heaven. In heaven all of the Lord's people will possess this intuitive knowledge that will enable us to recognize our friends and loved ones as well as the redeemed of all the ages.

The Rapture will be the beginning of a glorious reunion!

9. The Return (1 Thessalonians 4:17c)

...to meet the Lord in the air, and so we shall always be with the Lord.

At the Rapture, we will meet the Lord in the air. But after we meet the Lord in the air, what then? Where will we go? There are two answers to this question.

The Post-Tribulationist View: Up and Back Down Again

First, there's the post-Tribulationist view, which says that we go up to meet Christ in the air at the Rapture and then come right back down to earth with Him for His second coming. For post-Tribbers, the Rapture and Second Coming are really one event separated into two different parts by only a few moments. Post-Tribulationists base this idea on the meaning of the word *meet*, which is the Greek word *apantesis*. They maintain that this was a technical word used to refer to a group of people going out from their city to meet a dignitary and then immediately escorting him back to the city.

Does this make sense? Well, yes and no. A review of the uses of this term in the Septuagint (the Greek translation of the Old Testament) reveals that the word does not necessarily carry this technical meaning (see Judges 11:31, 34; 14:5; 15:14). According to the best known Greek lexicon, the word simply means "to meet."[9] For that matter, even if the word does mean to meet someone and then escort him back to the place you came from, there's nothing to prevent this from occurring seven years later when the church will come with Christ back to earth.

Also, we might ask this question: Why go meet the Lord in the air if we're going to come right back to earth with Him? Why not just wait here for Him? Meeting Him in the air seems pointless unless we continue on to heaven with the Lord, who comes out to meet us.[10]

That brings us to the pre-Tribulationist view.

The Pre-Tribulationist View: Up and Up to the Father's House

The pre-Tribulation Rapture view says that after we meet Christ in the air, we go up and up with Him back to His Father's house. 1 Thessalonians 4:17 doesn't say specifically where we go after we meet Christ in the air, but this passage is very similar in much of its wording to John 14:1–3. Note the amazing parallels in wording between these two passages:[11]

John 14:1–3	1 Thessalonians 4:13–18
trouble, v. 1	sorrow, v. 13
believe, v. 1	believe, v. 14
God, Me, v. 1	Jesus, God, v. 14
told you, v. 2	say to you, v. 15
come again, v. 3	coming of the Lord, v. 15
receive you, v. 3	caught up, v. 17
to Myself, v. 3	to meet the Lord, v. 17
be where I am, v. 3	ever be with the Lord, v. 17[12]

Since 1 Thessalonians 4:13–18 is so similar to John 14:1–3, and John 14:1–3 says that Jesus comes to take us back to heaven, then we can rest assured that Jesus will come for His own at the Rapture to usher us into the wonders of His Father's house in heaven.

We will be there in heaven with Jesus for the entire period of the seven years of the Tribulation and then return with Him to earth at His second coming.

10. The Reassurance (4:18)

Therefore comfort one another with these words.

Twenty centuries ago, this message was given to comfort believers who had lost loved ones before the Rapture. And it still comforts us today. Our loved ones who have fallen asleep won't miss the great reunion in the clouds. In fact, they'll get there first. But we'll be right behind them, and we'll all find ourselves together in the sky on that day when the trumpet sounds.

The truth of the Rapture is a source of supernatural comfort and hope to all of God's people when a believing loved one or friend goes home to be with the Lord. These words have certainly been read at thousands of funerals throughout the centuries and have brought the comfort, hope, and encouragement of the Lord to broken, bereaved hearts.

Rapture Wrap Up

Having considered these 10 *R*'s of the Rapture, I want to slow the film down even more and give a final frame-by-frame sequence of the events of the Rapture—a Rapture wrap up, so to speak.

Here's the sequence of the ten great events of the Rapture, frame by frame.

1. The Lord Himself will personally descend from the Father's house, where He is preparing a place for His glorious bride. He will bring with Him the perfected, disembodied spirits of believers who have died before the Rapture.
2. The Lord will give a commanding shout.
3. Michael the archangel will give a call to gather all the angels.
4. The last trumpet of the church age will sound, signaling the end of the church age, announcing Christ's arrival, and gathering His people to meet Him in the air.
5. The bodies of the dead in Christ will be raised incorruptible, imperishable, and immortal.
6. The perfected spirits and resurrected, glorified bodies of departed believers will be rejoined forever.
7. Living saints will be translated from earth to heaven.
8. Living believers will be instantaneously transformed in body, soul, and spirit. The new bodies will be

incorruptible, immortal, imperishable bodies that are fit for heavenly existence.

9. There will be a great reunion in the sky of all dead and living believers with the Lord.

10. Jesus will escort His bride back to the Father's house in heaven.

Jesus Is Lord!

There's one final observation about 1 Thessalonians 4:13–18 that I want to point out. In these six verses Jesus is called "Lord" five times over. Again and again the text highlights the lordship of Jesus Christ. I don't believe that there's another truth in the Bible that reveals the lordship of Jesus more powerfully than the Rapture.

He personally descends from heaven. He calls heaven His Father's house. He is called God in 1 Thessalonians 4:14. He gives one commanding shout, and all the bodies of the dead in Christ immediately respond to His call. These are bodies that have been in the ground for almost 2,000 years, bodies that had been burned to ashes, eaten by wild animals, or disintegrated in explosions. And not only that, He will transform millions of living believers—in body, soul, and spirit—and snatch them up to meet Him in the air.

And He does all of this in the amount of time that it takes to blink your eye.

That's power.

That's total lordship.

That's our *Lord*, Jesus Christ, the One who died in our place on the cross and rose again. Our powerful, gracious Lord and King.

3

THE RAPTURE
OF THE *CHURCH*

Now that we have an understanding of the main events and sequence of the Rapture, we need to pause and ask another very important question: Who will participate in the Rapture?

I'm sure you're thinking, *Well, that's obvious. Believers in Jesus Christ. Only those who have personally accepted Jesus Christ as their Savior from sin will be part of this great event. The Rapture is only for believers.*

That's right.

But is there any other qualification in order to be part of this great meeting in the sky?

I believe that there is.

The Dead "in Christ"

First Thessalonians 4:16 says clearly that at the Rapture "the dead *in Christ* will rise first" (italics added). This is a key phrase that tells us who will participate in the Rapture.

There have been millions of believers since the time of Adam, but believers before the Day of Pentecost, described in Acts 2, were not "in Christ." Only after the Day of Pentecost were believers placed in the body of Christ by the baptizing work of the Holy Spirit (see 1 Corinthians 12:13).

For this reason I believe that the Bible limits the participants in the Rapture to church-age believers, that is, people who have trusted in Christ as their Savior between the Day of Pentecost in AD 33 and the Rapture.

This present age is the church age. It could just as easily be called the age of grace or the age of the Spirit. It's the span of time in which we live right now, when Jesus is calling Jews and Gentiles and forming them into one body, of which He is the Head.

The church age will end with the Rapture when Christ's body, His bride, is called up to meet Him in the air. That's why the Rapture is often more specifically called "the rapture of the church." It only applies to believers in this era.

When Jesus comes at the time of the Rapture, believers will be found in one of two conditions: dead or alive. Believers who are alive on earth when the trumpet sounds will be immediately transformed and translated to heaven. Of course, all of these living believers will be church-age believers.

At the time of the Rapture believers who have died will be resurrected. They are referred to in 1 Thessalonians 4:16 as "the dead in Christ" or "Christians who have died." This indicates that the Rapture only pertains to departed church-age believers.

Since this is true, people often wonder what will happen to people who were saved before the beginning of the church age— people we often call "Old Testament believers"? When will they be resurrected and receive their glorified bodies?

The Resurrection of Old Testament Saints

God has a plan for His Old Testament saints as well. Two passages in the Old Testament place the resurrection of pre-church-age believers at the end of the Tribulation period. Notice in each of these passages that the writers specifically place the resurrection *after* the time of Great Tribulation.

> O LORD, they sought You in distress; They could only whisper a prayer, Your chastening was upon them. As the pregnant woman approaches the time to give birth, She writhes and cries out in her labor pains, Thus were we before You, O LORD. We were pregnant, we writhed in labor, We gave birth, as it seems, only to wind. We could not accomplish deliverance for the earth, Nor were inhabitants of the world born. Your dead will live; Their corpses will rise. You who lie in the dust, awake and shout for joy, For your dew is as the dew of the dawn, And the earth will give birth to the departed spirits. (Isaiah 26:16–19)

Another Old Testament passage that puts the resurrection of Old Testament believers after the Tribulation is in the book of Daniel:

> Now at that time Michael, the great prince who stands guard over the sons of your people, will arise. And there will be a time of distress such as never occurred since there was a nation until that time; and at that time your people, everyone who is found written in the book, will be rescued. Many of those who sleep in the dust of the

ground will awake, these to everlasting life, but the others to disgrace and everlasting contempt. Those who have insight will shine brightly like the brightness of the expanse of heaven, and those who lead the many to righteousness, like the stars forever and ever. (12:1–3)

Did you notice that Daniel 12:1 speaks of a future time of distress that will be the worst in all of human history? This must be describing the Great Tribulation that Jesus spoke of in Matthew 24:21. Then, in Daniel 12:2, the resurrection follows this time of trouble. And after that in 12:3 there's a reference to the coming messianic kingdom

It's clear, then, that the time of the resurrection of Old Testament saints is placed *after* the tribulation and *before* the millennial kingdom. It's sandwiched in between these two future events.

Daniel 12:1	The Great Tribulation
Daniel 12:2	The Resurrection of Old Testament Saints
Daniel 12:3	The Millenial Kingdom

Only church-age believers will be part of the Rapture before the Tribulation. God has a separate program for Old Testament believers. He will resurrect the bodies of Old Testament believers only after the Tribulation has run its seven-year course.

The Rapture of New Testament Saints

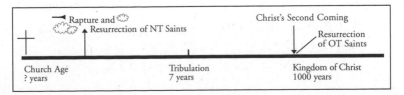

4

THE SEVEN RAPTURES
IN THE BIBLE

Many people find the idea of a Rapture—a snatching away of people to heaven without dying—difficult to accept. It just seems too strange and bizarre to be true. After all, they would say, nothing like this has ever happened before.

But that's actually not true. It may surprise you to know that there has been a rapture before. In fact, according to the Bible there have been at least seven rapture events in history.

To help us better understand the biblical concept of rapture, I want us to look together at what I like to call "the Seven Raptures of the Bible." Six of these rapture events have already occurred, and these six historical raptures strikingly foreshadow and help shed some light on the final Rapture that's still to come.

Let's look briefly at each of these biblical rapture events and see what we can learn about the final catching away.

The Three Old Testament Raptures

The Rapture of Enoch

The first rapture event in human history involved a man named Enoch, who lived before the flood. We find his story in Genesis 5. I like to call this chapter "God's Obituary Column," because eight times we read the phrase "and he died." God had warned Adam in the garden that the penalty for eating the fruit of the tree of the knowledge of good and evil was death (see Genesis 2:16–17). When Adam and Eve ate the fruit, they immediately died spiritually; that is, they were separated from God. But as time went on they also died physically.

Genesis 5 is the fulfillment of God's warning that sin brings death. This chapter is a compact catalog of the descendants of Adam through his son Seth, from creation to the days of Noah.

As you read Genesis 5:1–20, the phrase "and he died" are repeated over and over again like a sad refrain.

Adam died.

Seth died.

Enosh died.

Kenan died.

Mahalalel died.

Jared died.

But suddenly and shockingly, in the midst of the death and decay, there's a striking change in Genesis 5:21–24:

> And Enoch lived sixty-five years, and became the father of Methuselah. Then Enoch walked with God three hundred years after he became the father of Methuselah, and he had other sons and daughters. So all the days of Enoch were three hundred and sixty-five years. Enoch walked with God; and he was not, for God took him.

Enoch didn't die. God took him.

Enoch walked with God for three hundred years during the dark ages of spiritual corruption before the worldwide flood. And then God "took him" directly to heaven without dying. He was raptured to heaven. To make certain that there's no misunderstanding concerning what really happened to Enoch, Hebrews 11:5 confirms Enoch's rapture to heaven:

> By faith Enoch was taken up so that he would not see death; and he was not found because God took him up; for he obtained the witness that before his being taken up he was pleasing to God.

You may have heard the story that a child once told about God and Enoch going on a walk. He said that Enoch loved to walk with God every day. They would go on long walks together, talking like two friends. One day they had walked so far that God turned to Enoch and said, "Enoch, we've walked so far today that we're closer to My house than to yours. Why don't you just come on home with Me?"

Enoch is a powerful example to us of the importance of walking with God in difficult days. He also serves as a graphic illustration of the suddenness of the Rapture. He was there on earth one moment, and then "he was not." He was gone "in the twinkling of an eye" (1 Corinthians 15:52).

The Rapture of Elijah

The other Old Testament saint who experienced a rapture was the prophet Elijah. His rapture to heaven without dying is recorded in 2 Kings 2:1, 11.

> And it came about when the LORD was about to take
> up Elijah by a whirlwind to heaven, that Elijah went
> with Elisha from Gilgal....As they were going along
> and talking, behold, there appeared a chariot of fire
> and horses of fire which separated the two of them.
> And Elijah went up by a whirlwind to heaven.

The two men of God were just walking along, talking to
each other, and suddenly Elijah was taken up to heaven without
dying. All Elisha could do was look on in amazement.

Later Elijah appeared with Jesus and Moses on the Mount of
Transfiguration (see Matthew 17:1–3). In addition, according to
Malachi 4:5 Elijah will return to earth in some way during the
Tribulation period before the Lord's second coming: "Behold, I
am going to send you Elijah the prophet before the coming of
the great and terrible day of the LORD."

Will Enoch and Elijah Be the Two Witnesses in Revelation 11:3–14?

Since Enoch and Elijah were raptured to heaven without dying,
many people believe that they will reappear on earth during the
Tribulation period as the two witnesses in Revelation 11.

During the Tribulation period, Satan will have two hench-
men who will carry out his evil plan for the world: the Antichrist
and the false prophet (see Revelation 13:1–18). According to
Revelation 11:3–14, God will also raise up two special witnesses
who will minister on His behalf in the midst of the darkness and
devastation—and then be killed by the Antichrist.

Many of the early Christians, such as Tertullian, Irenaeus,
and Hippolytus, believed that the two witnesses will be Enoch

and Elijah.[13] There are several reasons why these men have been identified as the two witnesses.

Why Enoch? First, this was a godly man who never died, and the Bible says, "And inasmuch as it is appointed for men to die once and after this comes judgment" (Hebrews 9:27). Of course, this verse simply establishes the general truth that all must die. There will be millions of exceptions to this general rule at the Rapture when all the living saints are translated to heaven without tasting physical death. Enoch and Elijah are Old Testament exceptions to this rule. Second, Enoch was a prophet of judgment in the days before the flood who announced the coming of the Lord (see Jude 1:14–15).

And what about Elijah?

Five main reasons are given for identifying the mighty man of God as one of the two witnesses. First, like Enoch, he never tasted physical death. Second, he was present at the Transfiguration. Third, the Scriptures predict that Elijah will come before "the great and terrible day of the Lord" (Malachi 4:5). Fourth, God used him to prevent rain from falling for three and a half years just as the two witnesses will do (see 1 Kings 17:1; James 5:17). And fifth, like the two witnesses, Elijah was a prophet.

The fact that the two witnesses are not named in Revelation 11 causes me to reject this theory. Since the Lord doesn't tell us who they are, we really don't know for sure. On top of that, Hebrews 11:5 specifically states that God took Enoch up to heaven so that he would not see death. If he comes back as one of the two witnesses and dies it would seem to contradict that statement of the Lord.

I believe that it's best to view the two witnesses as two men who have never lived before whom God will raise up as his special witnesses during the Tribulation.

The Rapture of Isaiah

Isaiah 6 records God's personal call of the prophet Isaiah to ministry. Isaiah 6:1–3 says,

> "In the year of king Uzziah's death I saw the Lord sitting on a throne, lofty and exalted, with the train of His robe filling the temple. Seraphim stood above Him, each having six wings: with two he covered his face, and with two he covered his feet, and with two he flew. And one called out to another and said, 'Holy, Holy, Holy, is the LORD of hosts, the whole earth is full of His glory.'"

There are three different views of what might have happened to Isaiah during this call. First, some believe that Isaiah saw the Lord on His throne in the earthly temple in Jerusalem. While that's possible, there was no throne in that temple. Furthermore, the similarity of this passage to Revelation 4:8 indicates that this was God's throne, located in the heavenly temple, which was the model for the temple in Jerusalem. In Revelation God's throne is located in the heavenly temple (see Revelation 11:19; 15:5–8).

Second, others maintain that what Isaiah saw was only a vision—that he was not physically transported to heaven. But Isaiah 6:6 says that one of the heavenly beings touched Isaiah's lips with a burning coal. This indicates to me that he was actually present in heaven.

That brings us to the third view. I believe that Isaiah experienced a rapture—an actual catching up to heaven where he saw the Lord seated on His throne. If this interpretation is correct, then like Enoch and Elijah, Isaiah too was transported, translated, or raptured to heaven. Of course, unlike Enoch and

Elijah, Isaiah came back to earth, fulfilled his ministry, and eventually died.

The Four New Testament Raptures

There are four separate raptures mentioned in the New Testament,[14] three of which are past and one that is still to come in the future. In each of the four passages mentioning these events, the writers use the Greek word *harpazo* to describe the rapture event. I will italicize the English words that translate *harpazo* in each account.

The Rapture of Philip

The first New Testament rapture involved a man named Philip. The account is found in Acts 8:39–40:

> When they came up out of the water, the Spirit of the Lord *snatched* Philip away; and the eunuch no longer saw him, but went on his way rejoicing. But Philip found himself at Azotus.

Of the six people who were involved in biblical raptures, Philip is the only one who was not raptured to heaven. But he was physically snatched away from one location to another, about twenty miles away.

Just picture the scene in your mind. Philip has explained to the Ethiopian eunuch who Jesus is and how he can know Him personally. The eunuch believes in Christ and then asks Philip to baptize him in water. Philip baptizes the man, and when the Ethiopian official comes up out of the water, standing there dripping wet, he turns to say something to Philip, but Philip is gone.

He has simply vanished into thin air. Philip was instantaneously, bodily raptured or translated, not to heaven, but from one geographical location to another.

The Rapture of Paul

The rapture of Paul is one of the most incredible stories in the Bible. Second Corinthians 12:2–4 tells the story in Paul's own words:

> I know a man in Christ who fourteen years ago— whether in the body I do not know, or out of the body I do no know, God knows—such a man was *caught up* to the third heaven. And I know how such a man— whether in the body or apart from the body I do not know, God knows—was *caught up* into Paradise and heard inexpressible words, which a man is not permitted to speak.

Several have postulated theories about when this event occurred in Paul's ministry. But that's not Paul's focus. His emphasis is that at some point in his ministry he experienced a personal, individual rapture to heaven, where he received a revelation unlike anything that anyone has ever seen or heard. The experience was so incredible that the Lord gave Paul a "thorn in the flesh" so that he would not become arrogant and proud (see 2 Corinthians 12:7–10).

There are several people today who have written books about their supposed visits to heaven. They tell about being caught up to heaven and getting a guided tour by Jesus or Peter or some famous believer. When I hear about these accounts I always wonder why they never tell about their thorns in the flesh.

If Paul needed a thorn in the flesh after visiting heaven to keep *him* from becoming proud, you can rest assured that anyone else who visited heaven would need one too.

When Paul spoke of believers being "caught up" or raptured in 1 Thessalonians 4:17, he knew what he was talking about. He had experienced his own personal rapture. And he couldn't wait for all believers to experience what he had known.

The Rapture of Jesus

Most people probably have no idea that Jesus experienced a personal rapture. But the ascension of Jesus to heaven in Acts 1:9–11 is called a rapture. Jesus was "caught up" from earth to heaven without dying.

Jesus' ascension is referred to as a rapture in Revelation 12:5:

And she gave birth to a son, a male child, who is to rule all the nations with a rod of iron; and her child was *caught up* to God and to His throne.

In the context of Revelation 12, the woman who gave birth to Jesus is not Mary, but the nation of Israel. You will also notice that this verse skips over the years between Jesus' birth and ascension to heaven. It's a compact account of Jesus' life that only mentions His birth, His ultimate mission, and His ascension to heaven.

The key point is that Jesus was born on earth as the Messiah to rule the nations and that He was raptured back to heaven.

The Rapture of the Church

As we've seen, the first six raptures in the Bible have already occurred. The rapture of the church is the one rapture event that's still to come in the future. It's the one that these others fore-shadow or prefigure. And it's the one that this book is all about.

As we think back over the first six raptures, what do they teach us about the one Rapture that is still to come? Three important truths immediately come to mind.

First, the rapture of the church will literally happen. It won't be some symbolic event. Since the first six raptures in the Bible were literally fulfilled, we should expect for the final one to be literally fulfilled as well.

Second, the rapture of the church will involve a physical transfer of people from one place to another, namely from earth to heaven. The only rapture that didn't involve a transfer from earth to heaven was the rapture of Philip, but it too was a physical relocation from one place to another.

Third, the rapture of the church will happen suddenly, instantaneously. Enoch was there and then "he was not." The same was true of all the other raptures as well.

Conclusion

Now that we know at least the basics of the truth of the Rapture, let's turn our attention to the other great question that everyone asks about the Rapture: *When will it occur?* Will it be pre-Tribulation, mid-Tribulation, or post-Tribulation?

When it comes to the Rapture, this is the burning question in most people's minds. But which view is right? Is there any way to gain some degree of certainty on this controversial point? Does the Bible shed any light on this issue?

I believe that it does. And I invite you to join me for a clear, thorough, and thoughtful look at the timing of the Rapture.

PART TWO

THE TIMING
OF THE RAPTURE

By this time I hope that you can see that the real issue surrounding the Rapture is not whether there *will* be a rapture of the church, but rather *when* will it occur in relation to the Tribulation period.

All evangelical Christians believe in the Rapture. The Bible teaches it. We will be "caught up" to heaven someday, according to 1 Thessalonians 4:17. Nothing could be plainer.

However, there is wide disagreement about the timing of this event in relation to the Tribulation period. Simply stated, the key issue is this: Will the church go through any or all of the seven-year Tribulation before the Rapture occurs?

Inquiring minds want to know. This is *the big question* about the Rapture. It's clearly the most often debated issue about the rapture of the church.

But it's much more than just a theological, ivory-tower debate. There's a great deal at stake, depending on which view is biblical. Think about it. If the Rapture occurs in our lifetime, your future will be very different depending on which of these views is correct. Will you be here to see the Antichrist? Will you be forced to choose whether or not you will receive his mark on your right hand or forehead? Will you witness the carnage of the wrath of God poured out on the whole world? Or will you be in heaven during this time, experiencing a glorious fellowship and intimacy with the Lamb and His sheep?

Will you and I be here for none, half, or all of the Tribulation?

It's an important and sobering question.

For this reason, we will take the next eight chapters to investigate the timing of the Rapture.

5

THE FIVE MAIN VIEWS OF WHEN THE RAPTURE WILL OCCUR

When it comes to the timing of the Rapture, there are five main positions that are commonly held today. At this point I want to simply set forth a brief description of each of these views.

The Pre-Tribulation Rapture

Pre-Tribulationism teaches that the rapture of the church will occur before the commencement of the seven-year Tribulation period. The church will not be present on earth during any part of the outpouring of God's wrath. At some point after the Rapture the Tribulation will begin when the Antichrist enters into a seven-year treaty or covenant with Israel (see Daniel 9:27)

This view is the most popular of the Rapture views among

modern believers. It's been popularized in *The Scofield Reference Bible* by C. I. Scofield, *The Late Great Planet Earth* by Hal Lindsey, and the Left Behind series by Tim LaHaye and Jerry Jenkins.

The Mid-Tribulation Rapture

The mid-Tribulationist view says that Christ will rapture His church at the midpoint of the Tribulation. Believers will have to endure the first half of the seven-year Tribulation. Mid-Tribulationists maintain that the last half of the Tribulation is the time when God will pour out His wrath on the world. Believers will be caught up to heaven before this time of wrath.

Mid-Tribulationists defend their view by noting the frequent mention of three and a half years (forty-two months or 1,260 days) in Daniel and Revelation. But the main argument of mid-Tribulationists is the equation of the last trumpet in 1 Corinthians 15:52 with the seventh trumpet in Revelation 11:15.

One of the key problems with this view is that mid-Tribulationists can't even agree among themselves concerning where to place the Rapture in the book of Revelation. Among adherents of this view, there are at least three different theories regarding which passage actually references the Rapture: (1) Revelation 6:12–17, (2) 11:15–17, and (3) 14:1–4.

The Post-Tribulation Rapture

Post-Tribulationists hold that the Rapture will occur at the end of the Tribulation, right before the second coming of Christ back to earth. Believers will be raptured up to meet Christ in the air and then return immediately with Him back to the earth. The

Rapture and the Second Coming are basically viewed as one event, separated into two parts by a few moments.

Post-Tribulationists usually argue that while church-age believers will be present on earth during the Tribulation, God will protect them from the outpouring of His wrath. This view is the second most popular view after the pre-Tribulationist position.

The Partial Rapture

The partial Rapture position distinguishes between devout and worldly believers. According to this view, only faithful, devoted believers who are watching for Christ's coming will be raptured to heaven before the Tribulation. The rest of the believers will enter the Tribulation and be caught up during subsequent raptures throughout those dreadful days. One writer described the partial Rapture view like this: "All believers will go home on the same train, but not all on the first section."[15]

This view is based on New Testament passages that stress obedient watching and waiting for Christ (see Matthew 25:1–13; 1 Thessalonians 5:6; Hebrews 9:28; 1 John 2:28). It is the least popular of the Rapture positions, and I have what I believe to be six strong reasons for rejecting this view.

First, the Bible uses all-inclusive words like *we* and *all* when discussing the Rapture. This indicates that all believers will be raptured at the same time. "*We* will not all sleep, but *we* will *all* be changed" (1 Corinthians 15:51, italics added). First Thessalonians 4:14 says that when Christ comes he will bring with Him *all* "those who have fallen asleep in Jesus." The only qualification for participating in the Rapture according to First Thessalonians 4:16 is that a person be "in Christ." In other words, all you have to do is be a Christian. No other requirement is stated.

Second, the partial Rapture idea is inconsistent with the unity of the body of Christ that is formed by God's grace (see 1 Corinthians 12; Ephesians 2:14–3:6; 4:1–6, 12–16; Colossians 3:11, 15). All believers are equal in their vital union with the head of the body. When one part of the body goes, the rest of the body must go with it.

Third, all believers are promised exemption from God's wrath. The partial Rapture view creates a kind of Protestant purgatory on earth during the Tribulation. The only difference between this idea and the Catholic view of purgatory is that it would be on earth before death.

Fourth, this view seems to eliminate the need for a time for rewarding believers at the judgment seat of Christ (see 2 Corinthians 5:10). The Rapture itself would be our reward.

Fifth, if the timing of our translation to heaven depends on our own spiritual maturity or readiness, how ready do we have to be? What degree of maturity or readiness is required to make it in the first group? The Bible never says.

Sixth, every person I've ever met who believes in the partial Rapture view believes that he or she will be included in the first group that goes up before the Tribulation. They always believe in the pre-Tribulationist view for themselves. It's those *other* unfortunate believers who will have to go through varying degrees of tribulation before they can be caught up to heaven. But why believe that you are worthy for this special reward while other believers are not? It's inconsistent.

The Pre-Wrath Rapture

The pre-Wrath view contends that the Rapture will occur about three-fourths (five and a half years) of the way through the

Tribulation. According to this view, the catastrophes in the first three-fourths of the Tribulation are the result of the wrath of man and the wrath of Satan, not the wrath of God. God's wrath is not poured out until the seventh seal in Revelation. Believers will be taken up just before the wrath of God begins to be poured out on the earth. This view has been popularized by Robert Van Kampen in his book *The Sign* (1992) and by Marvin Rosenthal, who wrote *The Pre-Wrath Rapture of the Church* (1990).

To give you a visual picture of the differences between these views, here are the main five of these views in one chart.

Various Views of the Timing of the Rapture

1	**The Pre-Tribulational Rapture**	The Rapture will occur before the Tribulation period begins.
2	**The Mid-Tribulational Rapture**	The Rapture will occur at the midpoint of the Tribulation.
3	**The Post-Tribulational Rapture**	The Rapture will occur at the end of the Tribulation right before the second coming of Christ back to earth; believers will be raptured up to meet Christ in the air and then will return immediately with Him back to the earth.
4	**The Partial Rapture**	Faithful, devoted believers will be raptured before the Tribulation, but the rest of the believers will be left to go through the purging of the Tribulation.
5	**The Pre-Wrath Rapture**	The Rapture will occur about three-fourths (five and a half years) of the way through the Tribulation, when the wrath of God begins to be poured out on the earth at the seventh seal.

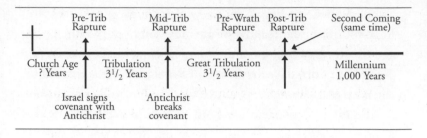

When Will the Trumpet Sound?

I hope I'm not confusing you. It's really not as complicated or intimidating as it may appear. Of these five views, the three most popular and commonly held are the pre-Tribulationist, mid-Tribulationist, and post-Tribulationist views. And if you want to boil it down even further, the two dominant views are the pre-Tribulationist and post-Tribulationist positions.

Warren Wiersbe is a well-known pastor and author who holds to the pre-Tribulationist position. But in his autobiography entitled *Be Myself*, Wiersbe tried to soften the debate on this issue and interject a little humor by taking a few lighthearted jabs at all three of the main views on the Rapture. Before we really get started looking at the Rapture up close, I thought you might enjoy this quote from Wiersbe's book:

> We are pleased to announce the first annual "Eutychus Pan-Prophetic Conference," which will meet for the first time. (Please note the hyphen.) There will be four conferences, each one devoted to a different view of prophecy. At no time will the delegates meet together since there is enough trouble in the world already without adding more. Also, we sell more books this way....The Pre-Tribulation Conference will assemble

in Dallas and last only one day, although it may seem like a thousand years. We are not revealing the day or the hour, so be prepared. There will be a special display of old prophetic charts, as well as a series of lectures on why pre-tribs write commentaries only on Daniel and Revelation and ignore the other 64 books of the Bible. All delegates who register will receive a free pocket calculator for figuring out prophetic dates.

The Midtribulational Conference will last exactly three-and-a-half days, Greenwich time. Several locations are under consideration, including Mt. Saint Helen's, Rome, and Chicago. Music will be provided by "The Uncertain Sound," a trumpet trio composed of students from three confused seminaries. There will also be a lecture on olive trees and candlesticks, plus a panel discussion on why midtribs write commentaries on only half of Daniel and Revelation.

Finally, the Posttribulational Conference will be held on the Mount of Olives and will last for seven days. White robes are included in the convention fee. We are anticipating a numberless multitude, so get your reservation in early. No lectures are planned, but there will be a great deal of singing—and maybe some tears and much sighing.

The management reserves the right to cancel all conferences should the Rapture take place.[16]

The Rapture Could Happen Today

In this book, as I've already mentioned, I want to focus on a clear, concise presentation of the positive evidence for the view that I hold, the pre-Tribulationist position. It's the only one of these five views that legitimately holds that the Rapture could happen today.

It's not my purpose in this book to look in-depth at the strengths and weaknesses of all the other views. There are scholarly books that do a fine job of that. But at a few strategic places sprinkled throughout the book, I'll point out some of the key weaknesses of the other views in contrast to the pre-Tribulationist view. I hope that this will help you see the solid foundation of the pre-Tribulationist position even more clearly.

P-R-E-T-R-I-B

So, what is the evidence for the pre-Tribulationist position? Do people hold to this view simply because it's more appealing than the other views? After all, being caught up to heaven before the terror of the Tribulation doesn't sound too bad, does it?

In the next seven chapters I want to present what I believe are the seven most compelling biblical arguments for the pre-Tribulation Rapture position—why I believe that the Rapture could happen *today*. I have arranged these seven points into a handy acronym that spells out *PRE-TRIB*.

Let's look carefully at the Biblical evidence and see if the case can be made for the pre-Tribulationist view.

6

PLACE OF THE CHURCH
IN REVELATION

If the church will experience any or all of the coming Tribulation, then one would naturally expect that the most in-depth, lengthy, detailed presentation of those dark days would include an account of the church's role during that time period. But, remarkably, in the key section on the Tribulation in the Bible, Revelation 4–18, there is absolute silence about the church.

And the silence is deafening.

The Greek word for "church" is *ekklesia*. This word occurs twenty times in the book of Revelation. In the first three chapters of the book of Revelation, the church is specifically mentioned nineteen times. The glorified Lord addresses seven letters to seven specific churches in Asia Minor: Ephesus, Smyrna, Pergamum, Thyatira, Sardis, Philadelphia, and Laodicea. In these letters the Lord gives detailed instructions and admonitions to the churches. But then suddenly, beginning in Revelation 4, John shifts from in-depth messages to the church to total silence about the church for fifteen chapters. Incredibly, the church is never mentioned once in Revelation 4–18. This absolute silence is striking and unexplainable if the church is to continue on earth during the Tribulation.

In Revelation 4:1 the apostle John, who is a member of the church, is called up to heaven and projected into the future in a kind of spiritual time machine. In the subsequent fifteen chapters, from Revelation 4 to 18, John looks down on earth as the events of the Tribulation unfold. But the church doesn't appear again until chapter 19, where she is pictured as a bride, beautifully adorned for her husband, who returns to earth with her glorious Bridegroom. This clearly indicates that the bride has already been in heaven for some time since she has "made herself ready" (Revelation 19:7). In Revelation 22:16, God gives the last mention of the church—*ekklesia*—in Scripture.

The place of the church in the book of Revelation is compelling evidence that the church will not be present on earth during the time when God pours out His fearsome wrath.

The Use of the Word Church in Revelation

Revelation 1–3	Revelation 4–18	Revelation 20–22
19 times	0 times	1 time (22:16)

What About the Saints?

Post-Tribulationists counter the above argument by noting that while the word *church* does not appear in Revelation 4–18, the word *saints* ("holy ones") occurs several times. These references, they insist, prove the presence of the church on the earth during the Tribulation (see Revelation 13:7, 10; 16:6; 17:6; 18:24). The problem with this argument is that there were saints in the Old Testament, there are saints today in the New Testament church, and there will be saints in the future Tribulation period. The use of the word *saints* to describe believers on earth during the Tribulation period tells us that there will be believers on earth, but it doesn't prove that they are church-age believers. The saints in Revelation are best described as Tribulation saints who will be saved during the seven-year period after the Rapture.

The Twenty-Four Elders

Post-Tribulationists further point out that if the church is not present on earth during the Tribulation, then she must be in heaven. They then ask the question, "What evidence is there in Revelation that the church is in heaven during the Tribulation?"

I believe that the church is referred to twelve times in Revelation 4–19 by the phrase "twenty-four elders" (Revelation 4:4, 10; 5:5–6, 8, 11, 14; 7:11, 13; 11:16; 14:3; 19:4).

There are four main views concerning the identity of the twenty-four elders: They are (1) angelic beings, (2) Israel, (3) the church, and (4) all of the redeemed—Israel and the church. Seven crucial clues in Revelation reveal that the twenty-four elders represent the church or body of Christ.

Their title

They are called elders (*presbuteros*), who in Scripture are the representatives of God's people. We get our English word *Presbyterian* from this word. I'm reminded of the little girl who came home from her Presbyterian Sunday school class, and her mother asked her what the lesson was about. The little girl replied, "We talked about heaven." "Well," her mother asked, "what did they say about it?" The little girl said, "The teacher told us that only twenty-four Presbyterians made it to heaven." (Hey, it's a joke.)

In the New Testament the elders of a church are its representatives. These twenty-four elders represent the glorified church in heaven.

Their number

The Levitical priesthood in the Old Testament numbered in the thousands (see 1 Chronicles 24). Since all the priests couldn't worship in the temple at the same time, the priesthood was divided into twenty-four groups, with a representative of each serving in the temple on a rotating basis every two weeks. While the nation of Israel was a kingdom of priests (see Exodus 19:6), only Aaron's sons were allowed to enter God's presence. However, all believers in the church are priests unto God (see 1 Peter 2:5, 9). This is yet one more evidence that the twenty-four elders are representative of the entire church of Jesus Christ.

Their position

They are seated on thrones, a specific promise that the Lord Jesus made to the church (see Revelation 3:21).

Their crowns

Scripture never depicts angels wearing crowns. Yet church-age believers will receive crowns at the judgment seat of Christ (see Revelation 2:10). Could this group include the saved from Israel before Jesus came to earth? No, because Old Testament believers will not be resurrected and rewarded until after the Tribulation is over (see Daniel 12:1–3).

Their clothing

The white clothing of the elders parallels the apparel of the redeemed in the church age (see Revelation 3:5, 18; 19:8)

Their praise

Only believers in the present church age can sing the song that the elders sing in Revelation 5:8–9.

Their distinction

The elders are clearly distinguished from angels in Revelation 5:11.

Where are these elders in Revelation 4–19? Do we find them on earth preparing for the Great Tribulation? No! They are in heaven, worshiping Him who sits on the throne and the Lamb. From their first mention in Revelation 4:4, the twenty-four elders are in heaven—judged, rewarded, and enthroned. Since the elders represent the church, this is one more indication that the church must be raptured to heaven before the first judgment of the Tribulation is unleashed in Revelation 6:1.

The only place you find the church in Revelation 4–19 is in heaven, as the twenty-four elders who are seated on thrones, dressed in white, crowned with crowns, worshiping the Lamb (see Revelation 4:4, 10; 5:5–6, 8, 11, 14).

7

RAPTURE VS. RETURN

Some students of Bible prophecy strongly object to the notion that the rapture of the church and the second coming of Christ are distinct events, separated by at least seven years. They contend that this is teaching two future comings of Christ, while the Bible only presents one event.

The New Testament, however, teaches that Christ will come *for* His church to escort her to His Father's house (see John 14:3). Scripture also asserts that He will come *with* His saints when He descends from heaven to judge His enemies and establish His glorious thousand-year kingdom on earth (see Zechariah 14:4–5; Matthew 24:27–31). I view this as one coming that will occur in two distinct phases or stages, separated by at least seven years.

The distinct differences between these two phases of Christ's coming are harmonized successfully by the pre-Tribulationist view, while other views of the timing of the Rapture are unable to accommodate the differences.

Here are some of the main verses that describe these two stages of Christ's future return to earth.

Rapture	Second Coming
John 14:1–3	Daniel 2:44–45; 7:9–14; 12:1–3
Romans 8:19	Zechariah 12:10; 14:1–15
1 Corinthians 1:7–8;	Matthew 13:41; 24:27–31; 26:64
15:51–53; 16:22	Mark 13:14–27; 14:62
Philippians 3:20–21; 4:5	Luke 17:20–37; 21:25–28
Colossians 3:4	Acts 1:9–11; 3:19–21
1 Thessalonians 1:10; 2:19;	1 Thessalonians 3:13
4:13–18; 5:9, 23	2 Thessalonians 1:6–10; 2:8
2 Thessalonians 2:1, 3	1 Peter 4:12–13
1 Timothy 6:14	2 Peter 3:1–14
2 Timothy 4:1, 8	Jude 1:14–15
Titus 2:13	Revelation 1:7; 19:11–20:6;
Hebrews 9:28	22:7, 12, 20
James 5:7–9	
1 Peter 1:7, 13; 5:4	
1 John 2:28–3:2	
Jude 1:21	
Revelation 2:15; 3:10	

The only surefire way to fully resolve this issue is to set what the Bible says about these events side-by-side to see if they are describing the same occurrence. You be the judge!

Dr. John Walvoord concludes that these "contrasts should make it evident that the translation of the church is an event quite different in character and time from the return of the Lord to establish His kingdom, and confirms the conclusion that the translation takes place before the tribulation."[17]

Both events mention clouds symbolizing a heavenly role, but other differences demonstrate that these are two distinct events. At the Rapture, the Lord comes *for* His saints (see 1 Thessalonians 4:16); at the Second Coming the Lord comes *with* His saints (see 1 Thessalonians 3:13).

At the Rapture, the Lord comes only for believers, but His return to the earth will impact all people.

The Rapture	The Return (Second Coming)
Christ comes in the air (1 Thessalonians 4:16–17)	Christ comes to the earth (Zechariah 14:4)
Christ comes for his saints (1 Thessalonians 4:16–17)	Christ comes with his saints (1 Thessalonians 3:13; Jude 1:14)
Believers depart the earth (1 Thessalonians 4:16–17)	Unbelievers are taken away (Matthew 24:37–41)
Christ claims His bride	Christ comes with His bride
Christ gathers His own (1 Thessalonians 4:16–17)	Angels gather the elect (Matthew 24:31)
Christ comes to reward (1 Thessalonians 4:17)	Christ comes to judge (Matthew 25:31–46).
Not in the Old Testament (1 Corinthians 15:51)	Predicted often in the Old Testament
There are no signs. It is imminent.	Portended by many signs (Matthew 24:4–29)
It is a time of blessing and comfort (1 Thessalonians 4:18)	It is a time of destruction and judgment (2 Thessalonians 2:8–12)
Involves believers only (John 14:1–3; 1 Corinthians 15:51–55; 1 Thessalonians 4:13–18)	Involves Israel and the Gentile nations (Matthew 24:1–25:46)
Will occur in a moment, in the time it takes to blink. Only his own will see His advent. (1 Corinthians 15:51–52)	Will be visible to the entire world (Matthew 24:27; Revelation 1:7)
Tribulation begins	Millennium begins
Christ comes as the bright morning star (Revelation 22:16)	Christ comes as the sun of righteousness (Malachi 4:2)

The Rapture is a translation/resurrection event; the Second Coming is not.

At the Rapture, the Lord takes believers from earth to heaven, to the Father's house (see John 14:3). At the Second Coming believers return from heaven to the earth (see Matthew 24:30).

The Rapture is an imminent, signless event, which, from the human perspective, could occur at any moment. By contrast, the Second Coming will be preceded by many signs (see Matthew 24:1–29).

The same event cannot logically be both signless and yet portended by numerous signs. This is flatly contradictory. The best harmonization of these two different events supports a pre-Tribulation Rapture (which is signless and could happen at any moment), while the many events taking place during the Tribulation are best understood as signs leading up to the Second Coming.

Conclusion

While both the Rapture and the return describe a coming of the Lord, these dramatic differences demand that they detail two very unique events at two separate times. It's simply impossible to merge the Rapture and the Second Coming into a single event that makes sense of the passages that describe them.

John MacArthur provides an excellent summary of this point in favor of the pre-Tributionist viewpoint:

> Scripture suggests that the Second Coming occurs in two stages—first the Rapture, when He comes *for* His saints and they are caught up to meet Him in the air (1 Thessalonians. 4:14–17), and second, His return to earth, when He comes *with* His saints (Jude 14) to execute judgment on His enemies. Daniel's seventieth week must fall *between* those two events. That is the only scenario that reconciles the imminency of Christ's coming *for* His saints with the yet unfulfilled signs that signal His final glorious return *with* the saints.[18]

Christ is coming *for* His saints. It could be today. Make sure you're ready for the meeting in the sky.

8

EXEMPTION FROM
DIVINE WRATH

Many people strongly object to the notion that the church will be raptured to heaven to escape the time of Tribulation on earth. They scoff at this as a form of Christian "escapism." After all, they argue, who are we to think that of all the generations of believers who have lived that we are somehow so special that we will be rescued from the coming time of trouble and tribulation?

Believers in every generation have faced trouble. Some—to this day—have faced terrible persecution and even martyrdom. Jesus Himself told His disciples, "In the world you have tribulation" (John 16:33). In Acts 14:22 the apostle Paul said, "Through many tribulations we must enter the kingdom of God."

Let me make it very clear that I *do not* believe that Christians are somehow exempt from the troubles of this life, even serious trouble. A cursory reading of the Bible would prove this point. True believers get ill, have family problems, deal with emotional stress, face persecution, lose their jobs, and die. We live in a fallen, sin-cursed world. But there is a vast difference between the troubles and tribulations of this life that we all face and the wrath of God poured out on a godless, sinful planet in the final years of this age.

It's the difference between tribulation (with a little *t*) and *the* Tribulation (with the definite article and a big *T*). We all experience tribulation. But the Bible says that we are exempt from *the* Tribulation.

Wrath or Rapture?

The Bible promises in several places that God's people are exempt from the coming wrath of God in the Tribulation period (see 1 Thessalonians 1:9–10; 5:9; Revelation 3:10).

But *why* are we exempt? What is there about the Tribulation that necessitates our absence from this time?

The nature of the *entire* seven-year Tribulation period is one of pounding judgment from God Himself against a rebellious world. The judgment of God begins with the first seal opened in Revelation 6:1 and continues all the way until the Second Coming in Revelation 19:11–21.

The Pre-Wrath and Mid-Tribulation Problem

Two of the other Rapture positions view the nature of the Tribulation very differently. Proponents of the "pre-Wrath Rapture" limit the time of God's wrath to the final part of the Tribulation. They believe that the wrath of God doesn't begin until the opening of the seventh seal in Revelation 6:12–16. According to them, all the destruction in the first three-fourths of the Tribulation is due to the wrath of man and the wrath of Satan.

Similarly, mid-Tribulationists argue that God's wrath is not poured out until the last half of this seven-year period of final judgment. They teach that Christians will be caught up just before the wrath of God begins. Most mid-Tribbers place the Rapture at the blowing of the seventh trumpet in Revelation 11:15–17.

The problem with these two views is that all nineteen judgments in Revelation 6–18 are God's wrath.[19] The seal judgments, opened at the very beginning of the Tribulation, are brought forth not by man or Satan, but by the Lamb Himself, the Lord Jesus Christ (see Revelation 6:1).

It is Jesus who opens the seals, and an angel calls each of the four horsemen to ride across the earth in judgment. To say that the wrath of God is limited to the last half or last fourth of the tribulation ignores the source of the seven seal judgments that commence the seven-year Tribulation. For that matter, even though the word *wrath* is not mentioned in Revelation until 6:16–17, the famine, sword, pestilence, and wild beasts in the first four seal judgments are often associated with God's wrath in other places in the Bible (see Jeremiah 14:12; 15:2; 24:10; 29:17; Ezekiel 5:12, 17; 14:21).

The very nature of the whole Tribulation period demands that Christ's bride be exempt from this entire time of trouble, not just part of it.

Is the Pre-Tribulationist View Just Escapism?

It's common to hear people say that pre-Tribbers are just escapists—that we're looking for an escape hatch that removes us from all the world's troubles. But the pre-Tribulation Rapture is not just escapism.

I like to call it "beliefism."

It's believing God's promise that we are exempt from His wrath. And when we understand what's in store for this world at the end of the age, we should be deeply grateful that we will escape the time of God's wrath.

I like what Billy Graham says in his book *World Aflame*:

> When I referred to the future God is planning, a student at the University of Hawaii asked me: "Isn't this a form of escapism?" I said, "In a sense yes; and before the devil gets through with this world, we are all going to be looking for the exit signs."[20]

The Rapture will be a great "exit sign" for the Lord's people from the time of tribulation.

The very nature of the Tribulation demands that God's people be rescued before it begins. To make sure that we fully understand the unique nature of this time in human history, let's pause for a moment to consider several important facts about the final years of this age.

The Nature of the Tribulation

In His gripping sermon on the Mount of Olives two days before He died on the cross, Jesus gave a blueprint of what the world will face in the time just before His second coming. He made it clear that this world will not become a better place in which to live. In fact, times of almost unbelievable difficulty are on the horizon.

Jesus said that the end of the age will be a totally unique time of terror. Nothing in all of world history will even compare to what is coming. It will totally eclipse all previous history in terms of hardship and trouble. Jesus said, "For then there will be a great tribulation, such as has not occurred since the beginning of the world until now, nor ever will" (Matthew 24:21).

Now that's saying a lot, because there have been some terrible times in the past, haven't there? Plagues that wiped out millions. Bloody battles. Famines. World wars. Earthquakes. The holocaust.

What is it that will make this future period of time that Jesus called the "Great Tribulation" so much worse than any other time in history? Two important distinctions.

The Scope of the Tribulation

First, the terror and destruction of the Tribulation years will not be limited to just a few locations. Its scope will span the entire globe—it will involve disasters of unimaginable horror. And there will be no place to hide.

As we've already noted, Revelation 6–19 contains the core biblical teachings on this time of future sorrow and woe. These fourteen chapters focus upon the terrible judgments of the end times. The main thread that runs through these chapters is the three sets of seven judgments that the Lord pours out on the earth.

There are seven seal judgments (see Revelation 6–8), seven trumpet judgments (see Revelation 8–10) and seven bowl judgments (see Revelation 16:1–12). These series of judgments will be poured out successively during the Tribulation.

Seven Seals.

Seven Trumpets.

Seven Bowls.

I believe that the seven seals will be opened during the first half of the Tribulation. The seven trumpets will be blown during the second half of the Tribulation. The seven bowls will be poured out in a very brief period of time right near the end of the Tribulation, just before Christ returns.

First Half of Tribulation	Second Half of Tribulation	Second Coming
Seven Seals	Seven Trumpets	Seven Bowls

Many times over, Scripture compares these judgments to birth pangs (see Jeremiah 30:4–7; Matthew 24:8; 1 Thessalonians 5:3). As the Tribulation progresses, like birth pangs these judgments will intensify in their severity and frequency.

Revelation 6–19 captures three crashing, crushing, devastating waves of God's judgment.

Seven Seal Judgments

First Seal (6:1–2) White Horse: Antichrist

Second Seal (6:3–4) Red Horse: War

Third Seal (6:5–6) Black Horse: Famine

Fourth Seal (6:7–8) Pale Horse: Death and Hell

Fifth Seal (6:9–11) Martyrs in Heaven

Sixth Seal (6:12–17) Universal Upheaval and Devastation

Seventh Seal (8:1–2) The Seven Trumpets

Seven Trumpet Judgments

First Trumpet (8:7) Bloody Hail and Fire: One-Third of Vegetation Destroyed

Second Trumpet (8:8–9) Fireball from Heaven: One-Third of Oceans Polluted

Third Trumpet (8:10–11) Falling Star: One-Third of Fresh Water Polluted

Fourth Trumpet (8:12) Darkness: One-Third of Sun, Moon, and Stars Darkened

Fifth Trumpet (9:1–12) Demonic Invasion: Torment

Sixth Trumpet (9:13–21) Demonic Army: One-Third of Mankind Killed

Seventh Trumpet (11:15–19) The Kingdom: The Announcement of Christ's Reign

Seven Bowl Judgments

First Bowl (16:2) Upon the Earth: Sores on the Worshipers of Antichrist

Second Bowl (16:3) Upon the Seas: Turned to Blood

Third Bowl (16:4–7) Upon the Fresh Water: Turned to Blood

Fourth Bowl (16:8–9) Upon the Sun: Intense, Scorching Heat

Fifth Bowl (16:10–11) Upon the Antichrist's Kingdom: Darkness and Pain

Sixth Bowl (16:12–16) Upon the River Euphrates: Armageddon

Seventh Bowl (16:17–21) Upon the Air: Earthquakes and Hail

It boggles the mind just to read this list. One-half of the earth's population will perish in just two of the nineteen Tribulation judgments. In the fourth seal judgment alone one-fourth of the world will die (see Revelation 6:8), and in the fifth trumpet judgment another one-third of humanity will perish (see Revelation 9:18).

The entire environment of the planet will be destroyed.

Revelation 16:19–21 graphically depicts the worldwide devastation: "And the cities of the nations fell....And every island fled away, and the mountains were not found. And huge hailstones, about one hundred pounds each, came down from heaven upon men."

Just think what it would be like to live on earth while all this is transpiring.

Post-Tribulationists believe that the church will be left here on earth to go through this entire terrible time of devastation, claiming that God will protect His people during this time. But with the global extent of these judgments, how could believers be spared? The world will be swallowed up by the tsunami of God's judgment.

The Source of the Tribulation

There is another key reason why the end of the age will be—by far—the worst time in the history of our world. When we look around us today at the suffering, destruction, heartache, and trouble across our world, we're seeing the results of the wrath of sinful man and the undying hatred of Satan. But in the Tribulation, *God Himself* will be pouring out His wrath on a sinful, rebellious world—on a scale not seen since the worldwide flood of Noah's day. All nineteen of the Tribulation judgments listed in Revelation are from the hand of the Almighty.

Read these verses from Revelation and note that God Himself and the Lamb are the source of this wrath against the world, from start to finish. In each verse I have italicized the mention of God's wrath.

And they said to the mountains and to the rocks, "Fall on us and hide us from the presence of Him who sits on the throne, and from *the wrath of the Lamb*; for the great day of *their wrath* has come; and who is able to stand?" (6:16–17)

"And the nations were enraged, and *Your wrath* came, and the time came for the dead to be judged, and the time to reward Your bond-servants the prophets and the saints and those who fear Your name, the small and the great, and to destroy those who destroy the earth." (11:18)

He also will drink of the wine of the *wrath of God*, which is mixed in full strength in the cup of *His anger*; and he will be tormented with fire and brimstone in the presence of the holy angels and in the presence of the Lamb. (14:10)

So the angel swung his sickle to the earth and gathered the clusters from the vine of the earth, and threw them into the great wine press of *the wrath of God*. (14:19)

Then I saw another sign in heaven, great and marvelous, seven angels who had seven plagues, which are the last, because in them *the wrath of God* is finished. (15:1)

Then one of the four living creatures gave to the seven angels seven golden bowls full of *the wrath of God*, who lives forever and ever. (15:7)

Then I heard a loud voice from the temple, saying to the seven angels, "Go and pour out on the earth the seven bowls of *the wrath of God*." (16:1)

The great city was split into three parts, and the cities of the nations fell. Babylon the great was remembered before God, to give her the cup of the wine of *His fierce wrath*. (16:19)

Standing at a distance because of the fear of her torment, saying, "Woe, woe, the great city, Babylon, the strong city! For in one hour your *judgment* has come." (18:10)

Sinful men will know that the worldwide judgments on the earth, seas, sun, and sky are coming from the hand of Almighty God Himself, and yet they will still not repent (see Revelation 6:16–17; 16:9–11). What a picture of the dark depravity of the human heart!

God's wrath will be unlike anything the world has ever seen. And we are compelled to ask the question: Why would God leave His bride on earth during this time? It makes no sense.

As J. F. Strombeck asks, "One is forced to ask, How could the Lamb of God die and rise again to save the Church from wrath and then allow her to pass through the wrath that He shall pour upon those who reject Him? Such inconsistency might be possible in the thinking of men, but not in the acts of the Son of God."[21]

The Language of the Tribulation

Another way to help us begin to wrap our minds around the horror of the coming Tribulation—and why the church must escape it—is to consider the graphic, vivid words that the Bible uses to describe these horrific days.

Old Testament Tribulation Terms and Expressions

Tribulation Terms	Old Testament References
Birth Pangs	Isaiah 21:3; 26:17–18; 66:7; Jeremiah 4:31; Micah 4:10
Day of the Lord	Obadiah 1:15; Joel 1:15; 2:1, 11, 31; 3:14; Amos 5:18, 20; Isaiah 2:12; 13:6, 9; Zephaniah 1:7, 14; Ezekiel 13:5; 30:3; Zechariah 14:1
Great and Terrible Day of the Lord	Malachi 4:5
Day of Wrath	Zephaniah 1:15
Day of Distress	Zephaniah 1:15
Day of the Lord's Wrath	Zephaniah 1:18
Day of Desolation	Zephaniah 1:15
Day of Vengeance	Isaiah 34:8; 35:4; 61:2; 63:4
Day of Jacob's Trouble	Jeremiah 30:7
Day of Darkness and Gloom	Zephaniah 1:15; Amos 5:18, 20; Joel 2:2
Day of Trumpet	Zephaniah 1:16
Day of Alarm	Zephaniah 1:16
[Day of] Destruction, Ruin from the Almighty	Joel 1:15
Day of Calamity	Deuteronomy 32:35; Obadiah 1:12–14
Trouble, Tribulation	Deuteronomy 4:30; Zephaniah 1:16
One Week = [Daniel's] Seventieth Week	Daniel 9:27
The [Lord's] Strange Work	Isaiah 28:15, 18
Time/Day of Distress, Anguish	Daniel 12:1; Zephaniah 1:15
The Indignation/the Lord's anger	Isaiah 26:20; Daniel 11:36
The Time of the End	Daniel 12:9
The Fire of His Jealousy	Zephaniah 1:18

New Testament Tribulation Terms and Expressions

Tribulation Terms	New Testament References
The Day	1 Thessalonians 5:4
Those Days	Matthew 24:22; Mark 13:20
The Day of the Lord	1 Thessalonians 5:2
The Wrath	1 Thessalonians 5:9; Revelation 11:18
The Wrath to Come	1 Thessalonians 1:10
The Great Day of Their Wrath	Revelation 6:17
The Wrath of God	Revelation 15:1, 7; 14:10, 19; 16:1
The Wrath of the Lamb	Revelation 6:17
The Hour of Trial	Revelation 3:10
The Tribulation	Matthew 24:29; Mark 13:24
[Time of] Tribulation	Mark 13:19
The Great Tribulation	Matthew 24:21; Revelation 2:22; 7:14
The Hour of Judgment	Revelation 14:7
Birth Pangs	Matthew 24:8

The Reasons for the Tribulation

Maybe you find yourself asking, "Why would God do this? Why would He judge the world that He created with such terrible severity? Why is such a time of unspeakable trouble necessary?"

Scripture lists at least five reasons for the Great Tribulation. These five purposes correspond to a specific group or person: Israel, the Gentiles, God, Satan, and Tribulation Saints.

1. To Purge Israel (A Purpose for Israel)

God will use the Tribulation to bring the Jewish people to their knees. During these seven fateful years, God will put the nation of Israel in a vice grip from which there is no earthly hope of deliverance. The rebellious nation will be refined by God in the fire of the Tribulation period.

"It will come about in all the land," declares the LORD, "that two parts in it will be cut off and perish; but the third will be left in it. And I will bring the third part through the fire, refine them as silver is refined, and test them as gold is tested. They will call on My name, and I will answer them; I will say, "They are My people," and they will say, "The LORD is my God." (Zechariah 13:8–9)

The Jewish people will cry out to God for salvation from their sins. They will implore God to split the heavens and come down to save them:

Oh, that you would burst from the heavens and come down! How the mountains would quake in your presence!…But we are not godly. We are constant sinners, so your anger is heavy on us. How can people like us be saved? We are all infected and impure with sin. When we proudly display our righteous deeds, we find they are but filthy rags.…And yet, LORD, you are our Father. We are the clay, and you are the potter. We are all formed by your hand. Oh, don't be so angry with us, LORD. Please don't remember our sins forever. Look at us, we pray, and see that we are all your people. (Isaiah 64:1, 5–6, 8–9, NLT)

God will mercifully answer this prayer of confession and will save a remnant in Israel. When the Jewish people repent and turn to their Messiah He will return in great glory (see Matthew 23).

2. To Punish Gentile Nations (A Purpose for Gentiles)

God will use the Tribulation period to punish the Gentile nations and all unbelievers for rejecting His Son.

3. To Prove God's Power (A Purpose for God)

About 3,500 years ago, the Pharaoh of Egypt mocked the God of heaven when he asked, "Who is the LORD that I should obey His voice to let Israel go? I do not know the LORD, and besides, I will not let Israel go" (Exodus 5:2). God heard this brazen challenge, and it's as if He spoke from heaven, saying, "Do you want to know who I am? Let me show you who I am!"

In the next eight chapters of Exodus, God took Pharaoh's challenge and proved to Pharaoh, his magicians, and all the people who He is. By the time God was finished with the ten plagues, Pharaoh was begging the children of Israel to leave.

In a similar show of foolish bravado, the Antichrist will totally deny the true and living God, declaring himself to be god. God will once again pour out His plagues to prove His power and vindicate His reputation—only this time on a worldwide scale. God will prove to a rebellious world that He alone is God.

4. To Portray Satan's True Character (A Purpose for Satan)

The Tribulation will also serve a purpose relating to the devil. God will use the events of those days to fully unmask Satan for what he is: a liar, a thief, and a murderer. When God removes all restraint, all that holds the enemy in check (see 2 Thessalonians 2:7), the nefarious character of Satan will be fully manifest as the world experiences the final firestorm from the dragon. Realizing that his time is short, the devil will pour out his venom with force and violence. "For this reason, rejoice, O heavens and you who dwell in them. Woe to the earth and the sea, because the devil has come down to you, having great wrath, knowing that he has only a short time" (Revelation 12:12).

5. To Purchase a Group of Believers (A Purpose for Tribulation Believers)

The Tribulation will be the greatest evangelistic tool in the history of man. The Lord will graciously use this terrible time of trouble to drive men to Himself in repentance and trust. The harvest of souls in these days will be more than anyone can number. Great revival will break out during the Great Tribulation.

> After these things I looked, and behold, a great multitude which no one could count, from every nation and all tribes and peoples and tongues, standing before the throne and before the Lamb, clothed in white robes, and palm branches were in their hands; and they cry out with a loud voice, saying, "Salvation to our God who sits on the throne, and to the Lamb."…Then one of the elders answered, saying to me, "These who are clothed in the white robes, who are they, and where have they come from?" I said to him, "My lord, you know." And he said to me, "These are the ones who come out of the great tribulation, and they have washed their robes and made them white in the blood of the Lamb." (Revelation 7:9–10, 13–14)

But did you notice in all the reasons for a Tribulation that one group is conspicuously absent?

The church.

The Tribulation is not for the church, the body of Christ, the

Lord's bride. There is no reason for us to experience God's wrath. In fact, to the contrary, we are promised exemption from it.

With this understanding of the nature, scope, source, and reasons for the Tribulation in mind, let's look together at some of the *pictures* and specific *promises* that indicate that the church will not go through any of the Tribulation.

Rescued from Wrath

While the Rapture finds no mention in the pages of the Old Testament, we see from the beginning that it is against God's nature and purposes to judge the righteous with the wicked. Genesis 19 records the rescue of Lot and his family from Sodom, when God poured out His wrath on the cities of the plain.

The rapture of Enoch to heaven before the flood is another illustration of this biblical principle (see Genesis 5:24).

The Pre-Tribulation Rapture in 1 Thessalonians

Four strong points in 1 Thessalonians indicate that the church will be exempt from the coming wrath of the Tribulation.

A Promise of Deliverance

First, verses 9–10 of the first chapter explicitly declare exemption from the coming wrath of the Tribulation: "For they themselves report about us what kind of a reception we had with you, and how you turned to God from idols to serve a living and true God, and to wait for His Son from heaven, whom He raised from the dead, that is Jesus, who *rescues us from the wrath to come*" (italics added). This passage clearly teaches that it is Jesus coming from heaven who delivers us from the wrath to come.

And the word *wrath* has the definite article in front of it. It's not just any wrath, but *the* wrath to come. This points to the specific time of wrath in the coming Day of the Lord. What's more, Jesus' coming for us is the means of our deliverance from that wrath. This strongly supports the pre-Tribulationist position.

First the Rapture

Second, in 1 Thessalonians 4:13–5:9, the order of events is striking. As we have already seen, 1 Thessalonians 4:13–18 deals with the rapture of the church to meet the Lord in the air.

Then, in 1 Thessalonians 5:1, Paul introduces a new subject with the phrase "Now as to…" (*peri de* in Greek). The Apostle employed this little Greek phrase in his letters as one of his favorite ways to change subjects. So, by using those words here, it's clear that he is finished focusing on the Rapture. But what's the next subject in verses 1 to 9? The day of the Lord, or the coming time of Tribulation:

> Now as to the times and the epochs, brethren, you have no need of anything to be written to you. For you yourselves know full well that the day of the Lord will come just like a thief in the night. (1 Thessalonians 5:1–2)

Why is this significant? Because of the order of the events. Which event is mentioned first, the Rapture or the Tribulation? It's the Rapture first, then the Tribulation. The Tribulation is depicted as a *separate* and *subsequent* event from the Rapture.

The order is clear.

1 Thessalonians 4:13–18	The Rapture
1 Thessalonians 5:1–9	The Day of the Lord (Tribulation)

The Rapture and the Day of the Lord can hardly be parts of the same event as post-Tribulationists maintain.[22] In one of most important prophetic passages in all of Scripture, the Rapture clearly comes before the Day of the Lord.

You *and* Them

Third, notice the interplay between the audiences in 1 Thessalonians 5:1–5. This is a subtle yet highly significant point. Read 1 Thessalonians 5:1–5 and notice the pronouns in italics (you probably never imagined that someone could get this excited about pronouns):

> Now as to the times and the epochs, brethren, *you* have no need of anything to be written to *you*. For *you yourselves* know full well that the day of the Lord will come just like a thief in the night. While *they* are saying, 'Peace and safety!' then destruction will come upon *them* suddenly like birth pains upon a woman with child, and *they* will not escape. But *you*, brethren, are not in darkness, that the day would overtake *you* like a thief; for *you* are all sons of light and sons of day. *We* are not of night nor of darkness.

Do you see the dramatic change in this setting between *you* and *we* (the believers) in the first and second person and *they* and *them* (the unbelievers) in the third person?

Don't blow right past this point. It's striking. The wording indicates that when the Tribulation comes there will be two groups of people, each exclusive of the other. One group will be raptured, and the other will face destruction.

The day of the Lord will come upon *them*, and *they* shall not escape (see v. 3). Then in verse 4 there's a sudden contrast: "But *you*...are not in darkness." *They* stand in sharp contrast to the believers in verses 4–11 who will escape.

This clear distinction between the unbelievers, who will not escape, and the believers, who will escape, is another strong indication that believers are exempt from the wrath of the Day of the Lord.

An Appointment to Keep

Fourth, 1 Thessalonians 5:9 says clearly, "For God has not destined us for wrath, but for obtaining salvation through our Lord Jesus Christ." In other words, believers in Christ have an appointment with salvation, not wrath.

Some maintain that this simply means that believers are not destined for the wrath of hell, but that we will be saved. I disagree—and I have two reasons for it.

First, the Thessalonians already knew that they weren't destined for God's wrath in hell. Paul had told them this very clearly in 1 Thessalonians 1:4. Second, in the context of 1 Thessalonians 5:1–8, what wrath has Paul just been talking about? Not the wrath of hell but the wrath of the Tribulation or Day of the Lord. In this context, *that* is the wrath from which believers will be delivered.

As Dr. John Walvoord says, "In this passage he is expressly saying that our appointment is to be caught up to be with Christ; the appointment of the world is for the Day of the Lord, the day of wrath. One cannot keep both of these appointments."[23]

We make our appointment for salvation and the Rapture the moment when we trust Jesus Christ as our personal Savior from sin.

Did the Apostle Paul
Teach the Pre-Tribulation Rapture?

After writing his first letter to the Thessalonians, Paul had to write them another letter within a few months. This letter is known in our Bible as 2 Thessalonians.

The problem this time was that someone had written a spurious, counterfeit letter to the church at Thessalonica claiming that it was from Paul. In this false, forged epistle the author had told the believers that they were already in the Day of the Lord or Tribulation period that Paul had discussed in 1 Thessalonians 5.

This bogus letter had deeply upset the Thessalonians. Their distress is evident in Paul's words to them in 2 Thessalonians 2:1–2: "Now we request you, brethren, with regard to the coming of our Lord Jesus Christ and our gathering together to Him, that you not be quickly shaken from your composure or be disturbed either by a spirit or a message or a letter as if from us, to the effect that the day of the Lord has come."

The Message paraphrase renders that second verse like this: "Don't let anyone shake you up or get you excited over some breathless report or rumored letter from me that the day of the Master's arrival has come and gone."

What does Paul's statement here indicate? I believe that it shows that these Thessalonian believers expected that they would be raptured before the Tribulation. Why do I say this? Think about it from the opposite angle. If the Thessalonians believed that they would have to endure the Tribulation before Christ's coming, then why would they have been so upset to receive a letter telling them that the Day of the Lord had come? They would have been excited, not shaken and afraid. This would mean that what Paul had taught them was being fulfilled. They would have faced the Tribulation with hope and endurance, knowing that the coming of the Lord was less than seven years away.

But that's *not* how they responded! When told that they were already in the Tribulation, they were "shaken from their composure" and "disturbed." The letter that they had received contradicted what Paul had taught them in 1 Thessalonians 4–5 and didn't square with what they'd previously been taught about the timing of the Rapture.

Getting that phony letter from someone claiming to be Paul and being told that they were already in the Tribulation caught them totally off guard. It shook them up and disturbed them. It caused a panic. It either meant that Paul had lied to them before about the pre-Tribulation Rapture, that they had totally misunderstood what he had said, or that the Rapture had already come and they had been left behind. Any of these scenarios was devastating.

There's really only one logical conclusion to be drawn from 2 Thessalonians 2:1–2. From Paul's previous teaching, these Christians believed that the Rapture would occur before the beginning of the Tribulation.

As Paul's second letter continued, he went on to show those men and women that they had been the victims of a false teacher and false doctrine. They most certainly were not experiencing "the day of the Lord," and their fears of having entered that awful period were groundless.[24]

Kept from the Hour

In the third chapter of Revelation, the Lord's promise of deliverance from the Tribulation period is very specific: "Because you have kept the word of My perseverance, I also will keep you from the hour of testing, that hour which is about to come upon the whole world, to test those who dwell on the earth. I am coming quickly" (3:10–11).

Notice four important things about this promise. First, the Lord promises to keep believers from the time of testing. The words *keep from* are the English translation of the Greek words *tereo ek*. Pre-Tribbers argue that this supports the notion of evacuation from the earth *before* the Tribulation. Post-Tribbers believe that this passage teaches protection of the church on earth *during* the Tribulation.

Let's take a closer look at that important Greek term *tereo ek. Tereo* is the Greek word for "keep, preserve, protect," and the Greek preposition *ek* means "out of, out from within." Those who oppose the pre-Tribulationist view argue that the word *ek* here means "through." That would make the passage read that the Lord will keep believers *through* the time of Tribulation, not *out of* it.

But if the Lord had meant that, why didn't He say it?

If He had meant "through," He would have used the Greek preposition *dia,* which carries this clear meaning. Furthermore, the only other use of *tereo ek* in the New Testament is in John 17:15, which says, "I do not ask You to take them out of the world, but to *keep* them *from* the evil one" (italics added). The usage of this identical phrase in John 17:15 supports the meaning of *ek* in Revelation 3:10 as "to keep from completely" or "out from within."[25] God doesn't keep His people through Satan—the evil one; He keeps us from him.

Also, if Revelation 3:10 is a promise of protection for believers through the Tribulation, then how does one explain Revelation 7:9–14, which presents millions of believers who are martyred during the Tribulation? It's much more consistent to understand Revelation 3:10 as a "keeping from" the wrath of

God during those days of judgment.

Second, the Lord promises to keep His people not just from, or out of, the testing, but from the very time or hour of testing. Our exemption is not just from the trials of the Tribulation, but from the very Tribulation itself. This strongly supports the pre-Tribulationist notion of *evacuation* out of the Tribulation, not the post-Tribulationist idea of *protection* through it.

Third, the time of testing that believers will miss is worldwide. It will "come upon the whole world." What is this time of worldwide testing? In the context of the book of Revelation, it is clearly the Tribulation period described in Revelation 4–18.

Fourth, after promising to deliver His people from the time of worldwide testing, Jesus gives the means of this protection in Revelation 3:11. How will this deliverance be accomplished? *"I am coming quickly."*

Putting these four points together, it is clear that the Lord will protect His people *from* the *time* of *worldwide* testing *by* His coming for them at the Rapture.

Well-known theologian Charles Ryrie gives an excellent illustration of the truth in Revelation 3:10:

> As a teacher I frequently give exams. Let's suppose that I announce an exam will occur on such and such a day at the regular class time. Then suppose I say, "I want to make a promise to students whose grade average for the semester so far is A. The promise is: I will keep you from the exam."
>
> Now I could keep my promise to those A students this way: I would tell them to come to the exam, pass out the exam to everyone, and give the A students a

sheet containing the answers. They would take the exam and yet in reality be kept from the exam. They would live through the time but not suffer the trial. This is posttribulationism: protection while enduring.

But if I said to the class, "I am giving an exam next week. I want to make a promise to all the A students. I will keep you from the hour of the exam." They would understand clearly that to be kept from the hour of the test exempts them from being present during that hour. This is pre-Tribulationism, and this is the meaning of the promise of Revelation 3:10. And the promise came from the risen Savior who Himself is the deliverer of the wrath to come (1 Thessalonians 1:10).[26]

Thank God. We will be kept from the hour of testing.

Calling the Ambassadors Home

Most Americans are well aware of what happened on December 7, 1941. It was "a day that will live in infamy." The Japanese bombed Pearl Harbor, inflicting heavy casualties on the U.S. Navy and crippling our Pacific fleet.

Many people also know what happened on December 8, 1941. President Franklin D. Roosevelt called on Congress to make a formal declaration of war against Japan and the Axis powers of Germany and Italy.

But do you know what happened on December 9, 1941? President Roosevelt issued an order calling all of the U.S. ambassadors home from Japan, Germany, and Italy. Before he unleashed the full wrath of the American military machine on those nations, he wanted to make sure that no American civilians were in harm's way. The wrath of America was for her enemies, not her own people.

In the same way, before God declares war on this godless world at the beginning of the Tribulation, unleashing His unmitigated wrath, He will call His ambassadors home.

Who are His ambassadors? Those who have put their trust in His Son, the true church of Jesus Christ. "We are ambassadors for Christ" (2 Corinthians 5:20).

God's wrath is not for the citizens of His heavenly kingdom. It's not for His own people. Make sure that you are one of His ambassadors before it's too late.

TIME GAP BETWEEN THE RAPTURE AND THE SECOND COMING

Another important argument for the pre-Tribulation Rapture is the necessity of a time interval or gap between the Rapture and the Second Coming.

Why is this so essential? Because the gap drops in like a puzzle piece that allows many of the end-time events that are predicted in Scripture to fit together in a logical and timely manner.

These end-time events can be harmonized by a pre-Tribulation time gap of at least seven years, while other views, especially those of post-Tribulationists, are forced to come up with scenarios that would not realistically allow for a normal passage of time.[27]

Here are three end-time events that point to a time interval between the Rapture and the second coming of Christ.

The Judgment Seat of Christ

The New Testament clearly states that all church-age believers must appear before the judgment seat of Christ in heaven. This event is often known as the "Bema Judgment," from the Greek word *bema,* which refers to a raised platform or step where awards were administered at the Greek games or the bar of justice where a judge presided.

Second Corinthians 5:10 says, "For we must all appear before the judgment seat of Christ, that each one may be recompensed for his deeds in the body, according to what he has done, whether good or bad."

The *people* at this judgment will be believers only. The context of Second Corinthians 5:10 clearly indicates that *we* refers to Paul and other believers. Everyone at the judgment seat of Christ will be a believer. Unbelievers will appear at a separate judgment—the Great White Throne judgment in Revelation 20:11–15. Everyone who appears before the Great White Throne will be condemned.

The *purpose* of the judgment seat of Christ *is not* to determine if a person is admitted to heaven or not. That issue was settled on earth the moment that we trusted Jesus Christ as our Savior from sin. God's Word teaches beyond dispute that those who belong to Jesus will never be judged for their sins (see John 5:24). "There is now no condemnation for those who are in Christ Jesus" (Romans 8:1).

The purpose of the judgment seat of Christ is twofold: to review and to reward. The Lord will review our conduct (see Romans 14:10–12), service (see 1 Corinthians 3:13), words (see Matthew 12:36), thoughts, and motives (see 1 Corinthians 4:5) after we became believers in Christ. Based on this review we will receive rewards from our gracious Lord.

The *place* of this judgment is apparently in heaven. We must each appear before the Lord.

The *period* of the Bema Judgment is apparently right after the Rapture. First Corinthians 4:5 says, "Therefore, do not go on passing judgment before the time, but wait until the Lord comes who will both bring to light the things hidden in the darkness and disclose the motives of men's hearts; and then each man's praise will come to him from God." This verse says that we will receive our rewards right after the Lord comes.

I find it interesting that Scripture gives no mention of the judgment seat of Christ in the detailed accounts connected with our Lord's second coming to the earth. Since such an evaluation like this would require some passage of time, the pre-Tribulation gap of seven years between the Rapture and the Second Coming would account for such a requirement.

Revelation 19:7–10 depicts the church as a bride clothed in fine linen, made ready for marriage to her groom, Christ. This beautiful apparel, we're told, represents "the righteous acts of the saints" (v. 8). Clothed in this way, the bride is prepared and ready to return with Christ to earth at the Second Coming (see Revelation 19:11–18). Given these things, it follows that the church would already have to be *complete and in heaven* (because of the pre-Tribulation Rapture) in order for the preparation that is described in Revelation 19 to take place. This requires an interval of time that pre-Tribulationism handles well.

Life in the Millennial Kingdom

The presence of believers in mortal, physical bodies during the thousand-year reign of Christ on earth presents yet another event or situation requiring a time gap between the Rapture and the Second Coming.

The Bible teaches that when Christ returns to earth He will establish His kingdom on earth, and it will last for ten centuries (see Revelation 20:1–6). Old Testament saints, church-age believers, and believers who died during the Tribulation will all enter the millennial kingdom in our new glorified bodies. Believers who come to faith in Christ during the Tribulation and live until the Second Advent will enter the millennial kingdom of Christ in their natural, human bodies. They will carry on ordinary occupations such as farming and building houses, and they will bear children, populating the messianic kingdom (see Isaiah 65:20–25).

Here's the problem: It would be impossible for people to enter the thousand-year reign of Christ in natural bodies if all saints were caught up at the Second Coming, as post-Tribulationists teach. Why? Because everyone would already have a glorified body. There wouldn't be anyone left in natural bodies to populate the kingdom.

However, because pre-Tribulationists have at least a seven-year interval between the removal of the church at the Rapture and the return of Christ to the earth, this is not a problem. Why? Because millions of people will be saved during the interval and will be available to populate the Millennium in their natural bodies in order to fulfill Scripture.

The Sheep and the Goats

Matthew 25:31–46 is a sobering picture of the judgment of the Gentile nations on earth that will occur right after the Second Advent of Christ, when He sets up His throne on earth. The people gathered at this judgment will be those who have survived the Great Tribulation. In describing this judgment Jesus said,

"But when the Son of Man comes in His glory, and all
the angels with Him, then He will sit on His glorious
throne. All the nations will be gathered before Him;
and He will separate them from one another, as the
shepherd separates the sheep from the goats; and He
will put the sheep on His right, and the goats on the
left." (25:31–33)

My friend Tim LaHaye says that this is why he knows that
God is a conservative—because He puts the sheep on His right.

Joking aside, at this great judgment event Jesus will divide
the Gentile believers into two categories: the sheep (believers)
and the goats (unbelievers). What this means is that when Jesus
returns at His second coming there will be both unbelievers and
believers alive on the earth.

Why is this significant?

Think about it. If the Rapture happens in conjunction with
the Second Advent, as post-Tribulationists say, and all living
believers are caught up to heaven to meet Jesus and escort Him
back to earth, then who are the sheep on earth when Jesus
arrives? Everyone left on earth would be goats. There wouldn't be
any sheep. They would have all just been raptured.

To state it another way, how would both saved and unsaved,
still in their natural bodies, be separated in judgment right after
the Second Coming, if all living believers are caught up at that
Second Coming?

There wouldn't be any need for Jesus to separate the sheep
from the goats when He gets to earth, because the Rapture
would have already accomplished the separation. On the other
hand, if the Rapture occurs *before* the Tribulation, there would
be time for many people to come to know the Lord during those

seven years of judgment. These Tribulation believers would be the "sheep" of Matthew 25:31–46 when Jesus returns.

Once again, the issue is solved by taking a pre-Tribulationist position with its gap of at least seven years.

A Post-Tribulation Rapture Is Meaningless

There's one final point that I want to make in connection with this discussion about an interval or gap between the Rapture and the Second Advent: Post-Tribulationists maintain that the Rapture happens in conjunction with the Second Coming. Believers will be caught up to meet the Lord Jesus in the air as He is coming from heaven to judge the world. Then they will come right back to earth with Him.

But this raises a very important question that often gets overlooked in this discussion: If God has miraculously preserved the church throughout the entire Tribulation, why even have a Rapture? Why bother? It's inconsequential. The Lord won't be delivering us from anything. There's really no purpose in it.

But if Christ comes before the Tribulation, His coming is filled with purpose. He will rescue us from the wrath to come.

Conclusion

Of all the views of the timing of the Rapture, pre-Tribulationism does the best job of handling the necessity of a time gap to harmonize a number of future biblical events. This requirement of a seven-year gap of time is just one more point that proves the likelihood that pre-Tribulationism best reflects the biblical viewpoint.

REMOVAL OF THE RESTRAINER

Second Thessalonians 2:3–8 outlines and describes in broad terms three important ages that take us from the present age to eternity.

The Present Age (Before the Rapture)	The Age of Restraint
The Tribulation Age (After the Rapture)	The Age of Rebellion
The Messianic Age (After the Second Coming)	The Age of Revelation

Let no one in any way deceive you, for it will not come unless the apostasy comes first, and the man of lawlessness is revealed, the son of destruction, who opposes and exalts himself above every so-called god or object of worship, so that he takes his seat in the temple of God, displaying himself as being God. Do you not remember that while I was still with you, I was telling you these things? And you know what restrains him now, so that in his time he will be revealed. For the mystery of lawlessness is already at work; only he who now restrains will do so until he is taken out of the way. Then that lawless one will be revealed whom the Lord will slay with the breath of His mouth and bring to an end by the appearance of His coming.

Amazingly, this present age in which we live is described as the time or age of restraint. There is something or someone who is restraining or holding back the full blast of evil that is to come when the Antichrist is unleashed. Think about it for a moment. If this evil day in which we now live is described as the time of restraint, what in the world will it be like when the restraint is removed? What will this world be like when all restraint against the Antichrist and his wickedness is taken out of the way? It will be like removing a dam from a lake—evil will overflow this world, swamping everything in its path.

Who Is This Restrainer?

The key question in this section of God's Word is, Who or what is this person or entity who is restraining the appearance of the Antichrist? Down through the centuries many candidates have been suggested. Here is a list of the most important ones:

1. The Roman Empire
2. The Jewish State
3. The Apostle Paul
4. The Preaching of the Gospel
5. Human Government
6. Satan
7. Elijah
8. Some Unknown Heavenly Being

REMOVAL OF THE RESTRAINER

9. Michael the Archangel
10. The Holy Spirit
11. The Church

St. Augustine was transparent when he said concerning the restrainer, "I frankly confess I do not know what He means." I can sympathize with Augustine, but I believe that there are several points that help us identify the restrainer.

1. The Greek word *katecho* ("what is holding him back," "the one who is holding it back," 2 Thessalonians 2:6–7) means "to hold back or restrain."
2. The one who is holding back or restraining is both neuter and masculine.
   Neuter: "what is holding him back" (a principle)
   Masculine: "the one who is holding it back" (a person)
3. Whatever it is it must be removable.
4. It must be powerful enough to hold back the outbreak of evil under the Antichrist.

In answering these four questions only one view is satisfactory. Just ask yourself this one question: Who is able to restrain evil and hold back the appearance of the Antichrist? The answer, of course, is God. In this case it is God, the Holy Spirit, who is at work during this age in and through God's people, the church.

Can the Holy Spirit Be Removed?

The main objection that's always mentioned when anyone identifies the restrainer as the Holy Spirit is that the Holy Spirit is omnipresent and can't be removed from the earth. I agree.

The Holy Spirit is the third member of the triune Godhead. He is omnipresent and cannot be removed from the earth. Moreover, millions of people will be saved during the tribulation (see Revelation 7:9–14). The Holy Spirit must be present on earth during this time to convict sinners of their need for salvation and bring them to faith in Christ just as He does today. The convicting, drawing, regenerating ministry of the Holy Spirit is essential for anyone to be saved, both now and in the Tribulation (see John 3:5; 16:7–11; 1 Corinthians 12:3).

I believe that the restrainer in 2 Thessalonians 2:6–7 is not just the Holy Spirit and not just the church. Rather, the one who holds back the onslaught of Satan is the restraining influence of God, the Holy Spirit, who presently restrains evil through the church.

In Acts 2, the Holy Spirit came to earth in a new capacity that He had not fulfilled before. He was present on earth before that time. The Spirit was present during creation according to Genesis 1:2 and was on earth all during Old Testament times to convict sinners and uniquely empower certain ones of God's people. But on the Day of Pentecost He came to earth with a new ministry: to indwell each individual believer and the church as a whole. He came to earth in a new capacity or new ministry. And the presence of the Spirit in all believers individually and corporately is the means that God uses in this age to restrain evil. That restraining influence will be here as long as the church is here.

The return of the Holy Spirit to heaven will not be a complete withdrawal from earth, but a return in the sense that He came at the very beginning of the church age.

The Spirit and the Church

There are four key reasons for identifying the one who holds evil back as the restraining ministry of the Holy Spirit through the church.

1. This restraint requires omnipotent power.
2. This is the only view that adequately explains the change in gender in 2 Thessalonians 2:6–7. In Greek the word *pneuma* (Spirit) is neuter. But the Holy Spirit is also consistently referred to by the masculine pronoun *He*, especially in John 14–16.
3. The Holy Spirit is spoken of in Scripture as restraining sin and evil in the world (see Genesis 6:3) and in the heart of the believer (see Galatians 5:16–17).
4. The church and its mission of proclaiming and portraying the gospel is the primary instrument that the Holy Spirit uses in this age to restrain evil. We are the salt of the earth and the light of the world (see Matthew 5:13–16). We are the temple of the Holy Spirit, both individually and corporately (see 1 Corinthians 3:17; 6:19; Ephesians 2:21–22).

The restrainer then is the restraining influence and ministry of the Holy Spirit indwelling and working through His people in this present age. Therefore, when the Spirit goes, the church must go with Him.

The great Bible teacher and expositor Donald Grey Barnhouse summarizes this view:

Well, what is keeping the Antichrist from putting in his appearance on the world stage? *You* are! You and every other member of the body of Christ on earth. The presence of the church of Jesus Christ is the restraining force that refuses to allow the man of lawlessness to be revealed. True, it is the Holy Spirit who is the real restrainer. But as both 1 Corinthians 3:16 and 6:19 teach, the Holy Spirit indwells the believer. The believer's body is the temple of the Spirit of God. Put all believers together then, with the Holy Spirit indwelling each of us, and you have a formidable restraining force.

For when the church is removed at the rapture, the Holy Spirit goes with the church insofar as His restraining power is concerned. His work in this age of grace will be ended. Henceforth, during the Great Tribulation, the Holy Spirit will still be here on earth, of course— for how can you get rid of God?—but He will not be indwelling believers as He does now. Rather, he will revert to His Old Testament ministry of "coming upon" special people.[28]

When the Rapture occurs, the Spirit-indwelt church and its restraining influence will be removed, and Satan will put his plan into full swing by bringing his man onto center stage to take control of the world.

The removal of the restrainer is another strong argument for the pre-Tribulation Rapture.

11

IMMINENCY: THE ANY-MOMENT RAPTURE

People often ask me why I believe in the pre-Tribulation Rapture. As you have already seen, there are many reasons why I believe that this view best represents New Testament teaching. But I believe that the strongest and probably the simplest reason is what is often called imminency.

What do we mean by the word *imminent*? What is the biblical definition of this doctrine?

We employ the English word *imminent* most often to simply mean "soon" or "near." But when it is used as a theological term, pre-Tribulationists mean something different.

When pre-Tribulationists use this word, we have three main ideas in mind. First, imminency means that, from the human perspective, the Rapture could occur at any moment. Other events *may* take place before the Rapture, but no event *must* precede it. After all, if some event must happen before the Rapture, then the Rapture could not happen at any moment. It could not be imminent.[29] An imminent event, according to Charles Ryrie, is one that is "impending, hanging over one's head, ready to take place. An imminent event is one that is always ready to take place."[30]

Second, imminency means that the Rapture is a signless event. Since our Lord's call for believers to meet Him in the clouds is an any-moment event, then it follows that one must be ready for it at any time, without any signs or warning. If signs have to precede it, then it can't occur at any moment. The signs of Christ's coming in the New Testament, such as those in Matthew 24, are signs of the Second Coming of Christ, not signs of the Rapture.

Third, imminency means that the Rapture is certain to happen, but not necessarily soon. Prophecy expert Renald Showers clarifies this point:

> "A person cannot legitimately say that an imminent event will happen soon. The term 'soon' implies that an event must take place 'within a short time (after a particular point of time specified or implied).' By contrast, an imminent event may take place within a short time, but it does not have to do so in order to be imminent. As I hope you can see by now, 'imminent' is not equal to soon."[31]

Imminency, therefore, combines two key conditions: certainty and uncertainty. An imminent event is one that is certain to occur, but its actual timing is uncertain.[32] For these reasons, those who believe in the pre-Tribulation Rapture should carefully avoid saying things like "Jesus is coming soon!" or "The Rapture is going to happen very soon." It may happen soon, but it may not. We simply don't know for sure.

What we ought to say instead is, "From our human perspective, the Rapture can happen at any moment—it could happen today." I think that this more accurately reflects the biblical teaching of imminency.

Imminency in the New Testament

One question that you might be asking at this point is, "Does the New Testament really teach the idea of imminency? Where do we find this idea in the Bible?" Let's consider some of the key passages that teach this truth:

- 1 Corinthians 1:7: "...awaiting eagerly the revelation of our Lord Jesus Christ."
- 1 Corinthians 16:22: "Maranatha."
- Philippians 3:20: "For our citizenship is in heaven, from which also we eagerly wait for a Savior, the Lord Jesus Christ."
- Philippians 4:5: "The Lord is near."
- 1 Thessalonians 1:10: "...to wait for His Son from heaven..."
- Titus 2:13: "...looking for the blessed hope and the appearing of the glory of our great God and Savior, Christ Jesus."
- Hebrews 9:28: "So Christ...will appear a second time for salvation without reference to sin, to those who eagerly await Him."
- James 5:7–9: "Therefore be patient, brethren, until the coming of the Lord...for the coming of the Lord is near...behold, the Judge is standing right at the door."

- 1 Peter 1:13: "Fix your hope completely on the grace to be brought to you at the revelation of Jesus Christ."
- Jude 1:21: "...waiting anxiously for the mercy of our Lord Jesus Christ to eternal life."
- Revelation 3:11; 22:7, 12, 20: "I am coming quickly."
- Revelation 22:17, 20: "The Spirit and the bride say, 'Come.' And let the one who hears say, 'Come.'...He who testifies to these things says, 'Yes, I am coming quickly.' Amen. Come, Lord Jesus."

All of these Scriptures refer to the Rapture and speak of it as though it could occur at any moment. It's something that we're always to be looking for, because we're looking for a *person*—the Lord Jesus Christ—not signs or an event. We are "wait[ing] for His Son from heaven" (1 Thessalonians 1:10).

Jesus May Come Today!

One of my friends once said that he believes so strongly in the pre-Tribulation Rapture that he always eats his dessert first when he sits at the table for a meal. Now that's putting your theology into practice!

I think that my friend has the right idea. Why? Because only the pre-Tribulationist position allows for an imminent, any-moment, signless coming of Christ for His own. Only those who believe in a pre-Tribulation Rapture can honestly say, "Jesus may come today." Since the Tribulation period has not started yet, for mid-Tribbers the Rapture must be at least three and a half years away, for pre-Wrathers it must be at least five and a half years away, and for post-Tribbers it is at least seven years down the road.

The New Testament truth of the any-moment coming of Christ fills us with hope, anticipation, and a strong motivation for godly living. Believers should live with this hope—the hope that Jesus may come today—every day! Only the pre-Tribulationist view allows for this blessed hope (see Titus 2:13).

One of my colleagues recently related a story to me about the great expositor Donald Grey Barnhouse. He said that Dr. Barnhouse loved to sing that old hymn "Is It the Crowning Day?":

> *Jesus may come today, Glad day! Glad day!*
> *And I would see my friend;*
> *Dangers and troubles would end*
> *If Jesus should come today.*
> *Glad day! Glad day! Is it the crowning day?*
> *I'll live for today, nor anxious be,*
> *Jesus, my Lord, I soon shall see;*
> *Glad day! Glad day! Is it the crowning day?*

To drive home the point that only the pre-Tribulationist view is consistent with imminency, Dr. Barnhouse loved to point out that if mid-Tribbers or post-Tribbers sang this song they would have to say,

> *Jesus can't come today, Sad day! Sad day!*
> *And I won't see my friend;*
> *Dangers and troubles won't end*
> *Because Jesus can't come today.*
> *Sad day! Sad day! Today is not*
> *the crowning day?*
> *I won't live for today, and anxious I'll be,*

The Beast and the False Prophet I soon shall see,
Sad day! Sad day!
Today is not the crowning day?

We may get a laugh out of this parody, but it rings true. The pre-Tribulationist position is the only view that honestly holds that Jesus could come today.

A Simple Test

One time I asked the late Dr. John Walvoord to tell me the simplest, easiest way to prove the truth of the pre-Tribulation Rapture to another person. He responded without hesitation. "All you have to do," he told me, "is ask a person two simple questions. First, 'Do you believe that Jesus is coming back to rapture His people to heaven?' If the person says, 'Yes,' then pose a second question.: 'Do you believe that the Rapture could occur at any moment? That Jesus could come back today?' If the person responds, 'Yes,' then tell the person, 'You are a pre-Tribulationist!'"

He was absolutely correct.

You see, only a pre-Tribber can get up in the morning, look up to the sky, and whisper, "Maybe today, Lord…maybe today."

Maranatha!

The early church had a special watchword or password that they used to identify themselves to one another. It also served as a joyful greeting within the family of God. This word, appearing only once in the New Testament, was *Maranatha* (see 1 Corinthians 16:22). It's an Aramaic word that the pagans who spoke Greek couldn't understand. It consists of three Aramaic words: *Mar* (Lord), *ana* (our), and *tha* (come). In a sense, it's a one-word prayer: "Our Lord, come."

Obviously, *Maranatha* only makes sense in light of the imminent coming of Christ. Why say, "Maranatha" ("our Lord, come") if you know that Christ *can't* come for at least three and a half to seven years, as the other views of the Rapture teach?

It's beautiful that the early church coined this greeting to reflect their hourly hope, eager expectation, and ardent anticipation of the Rapture. No doubt this expectation was a powerful incentive for personal purity and evangelism.

Think of how it would change the church today if we were to return to this form of greeting our brothers and sisters in Christ. Think of how it would change our lives if this simple watchword was always on the lips of an expectant people.[33]

Maranatha!

12

BLESSED HOPE

In all the debate, theological sniping, and sometimes con-
tentious disagreement that takes place over the timing of the
Rapture, we must never lose sight of one simple truth: The
New Testament teaching on this glorious event is intended to
bless and comfort the Lord's people. God wants us to long for
and look forward to that moment when the trumpet sounds
and we meet our Lord and our loved ones in the air.

Here are three of the key passages that present the blessing
and comfort of the Rapture:

In John 14:1–3, Jesus said,

> "Do not let your heart be troubled; believe in God,
> believe also in Me. In My Father's house are many
> dwelling places; if it were not so, I would have told
> you; for I go to prepare a place for you. If I go and
> prepare a place for you, I will come again and
> receive you to Myself, that where I am, there you
> may be also."

Titus 2:13 says, "...looking for the blessed hope and the appearing of the glory of our great God and Savior, Christ Jesus."

In 1 Thessalonians 4:18, after describing the Rapture, Paul concludes with this gentle reminder: "Therefore comfort one another with these words."

A soothing balm for troubled hearts, the doctrine of the Rapture provides reassurance and consolation for the Lord's people.

Blessing or Blasting?

Stop and think about this for a moment. If Paul taught a mid-Tribulationist, pre-Wrath, or post-Tribulationist view, would the thought of the upcoming Rapture really be that comforting? If God's people have to endure three and a half years, five and a half years, or all seven years of the most horrible days that the world has ever known before He comes...well, where's the comfort in that?

If we must face the Tribulation before He comes, Jesus would have to change the words "Do not let your heart be troubled" in John 14:1 to "Let your heart be troubled." I don't know about you, but knowing that I had to live through the Tribulation would be troubling to say the least.

Ask yourself this simple question: How comforting would it be to know that Jesus was coming after three and a half or seven years of hell on earth?

Try to imagine this. You're standing at the graveside of a loved one. You hear the pastor read the beautiful words in 1 Thessalonians 4:13–17, and then he says, "And after we endure part or all of the Tribulation, Jesus will come and rapture us to heaven and reunite us to our loved ones—comfort one another with these words."

Could you honestly get excited about the Rapture if you knew that you had to endure a time on earth when all the nineteen judgments of Revelation 6–16—the terrible wrath of a mighty God—were being poured out? Do you find any reassurance or consolation in a time when the Antichrist will be enforcing his mark and you and your family would be denied the right to buy or sell?

If that's what the Apostle meant by "*comfort* one another" (italics added), then maybe we need a new definition for the word.

A Quick Comparison

Let's suppose for a moment that the Rapture will occur at the middle or the end of the Tribulation. I know that's a scary thought, but bear with me for a minute.

What would we expect to find in 1 Thessalonians 4:13–18? And how does this compare with what we find in these verses?

First, we would expect the Thessalonians to be rejoicing that their loved ones had already died and gone to heaven and wouldn't have to endure the terror of the Tribulation. In this passage, however, the believers are grieving because they fear that their loved ones will miss the Rapture. Only a pre-Tribulation Rapture makes sense out of their grief.

Second, we would expect the Thessalonians to be upset about their own impending trial in the Tribulation rather than sorrowing over their deceased loved ones. We would expect them to be asking for details about the Tribulation and the Antichrist. But it's obvious that the Thessalonians had neither questions nor fear about the coming day of wrath or the Antichrist. Why? They were looking for Christ, not the Antichrist.

Third, we would expect Paul, in view of their grief over their deceased loved ones, to remind them that their present grief was inconsequential in light of the future time of trouble that's coming. But there's not even a hint of any impending Tribulation for them.

What we find in 1 Thessalonians 4 fits the pre-Tribulationist position like a glove, but it's totally incompatible with either mid-Tribulationism or post-Tribulationism.[34]

The blessed hope of the Rapture is that Jesus will come and take us to be with Him forever before the time of worldwide devastation is unleashed. And what a comfort and blessing it is!

PART
THREE

QUESTIONS ABOUT
THE RAPTURE

The idea of the any-moment Rapture raises many questions in people's minds. As I've explained the truth and timing of this incredible episode on God's schedule of end-time events, I've tried to answer many of the commonly asked questions.

But I'm sure that there are more questions. There always are! And while I certainly don't profess to have all the answers about the Rapture—or any other area of prophecy, for that matter—I want to give my best effort to tackle some of the nagging questions that may have occurred to you while you were reading the first twelve chapters of this book.

Each of the next ten sections will answer a basic question that people like you and me have about the pre-Tribulation Rapture.

13

TEN COMMONLY ASKED QUESTIONS ABOUT THE RAPTURE

Question #1: Is the Pre-Tribulation Rapture a Recent Invention?

One of the constant charges leveled against the pre-Tribulation Rapture is that it can't be right because it only came into being around 1830 through the ministry and teaching of an Irish Brethren preacher named J. N. Darby.

I've heard and read this argument scores of times. It's one of the standard, boilerplate arguments against the pre-Tribulation Rapture. And until recently it went unanswered. But in the last few years several discoveries have put this argument to rest once and for all.

A careful study of church history clearly shows that the pre-Tribulation Rapture position has strong historical precedent. It *was not* created by J. N. Darby in the 1830s. There are several important voices from church history who held to the pre-Tribulation position long before the 1830s. Let's consider three of these witnesses.

Ancient End-Times Sermon

A clear statement of the pre-Tribulation Rapture position can be found as early as the fourth to the seventh century AD. A sermon preached by Pseudo-Ephraem entitled "On the Last Times, the Antichrist, and the End of the World, or Sermon on the End of the World" includes a concept very similar to the pre-Tribulation Rapture more than one thousand years before the writings of J. N. Darby. Considered "one of the most interesting apocalyptic texts of the early Middle Ages,"[35] the sermon contains just under 1,500 words.

Concerning the timing of the Rapture the sermon reads:

> We ought to understand thoroughly therefore, my brothers, what is imminent or overhanging....Why therefore do we not reject every care of earthly actions and prepare ourselves for the meeting of the Lord Jesus Christ, so that he may *draw us from* the confusion, which overwhelms all the world?...For all the saints and elect of God are gathered together *before the tribulation*, which is to come, and are taken to the Lord, in order that they may not see at any time the confusion which overwhelms the world because of our sins. (italics added)

According to prophecy scholars Thomas Ice and Timothy Demy, Pseudo-Ephraem clearly presents at least three important features found in modern pre-Tribulationism:

134 QUESTIONS ABOUT THE RAPTURE

(1) There are two distinct comings: the return of Christ to rapture the saints, followed later by Christ's Second Advent to the earth, (2) a defined interval between the two comings, in this case three and one-half years, and (3) a clear statement that Christ will remove the church from the world before the Tribulation.[36]

The fact that Pseudo-Ephraem placed the rapture three and a half years before the Tribulation is not an argument for mid-Tribulationism because it appears that for him the whole tribulation was only three and a half years in duration.

We can say with assurance, then, that the pre-Tribulation Rapture position is not a recent view. It was held and preached possibly as early as AD 373. The alleged "novelty" of this view should no longer be used as an argument against it.

But Pesudo-Ephraem is not alone. There's testimony from yet another ancient witness.

Brother Dolcino

In AD 1260, a man named Gerard Sagarello founded a group known as the Apostolic Brethren in northern Italy. He founded this order after he was turned down for membership by the Franciscan order.

At that time it was against church law to form any new ecclesiastical order, so the Apostolic Brethren were subjected to severe persecution. In 1300, Gerard was burned at the stake, and a man named Brother Dolcino took over leadership of the movement. Under his hand, the order grew and eventually numbered in the thousands. End-time prophecy evidently held an important place in the study and teaching of the Apostolic Brethren.

Brother Dolcino died in 1307, and in 1316 an anonymous notary of the diocese of Vercelli in northern Italy wrote a brief treatise in Latin that set forth the deeds and beliefs of the Apostolic Brethren. This treatise was called *The History of Brother Dolcino*.

At one point in this treatise the following paragraph appears:

Again, [Dolcino believed and preached and taught] that within those three years Dolcino himself and his followers will preach the coming of the Antichrist. And that the Antichrist was coming into this world within the bounds of the said three and a half years; and after he had come, then *he [Dolcino] and his followers would be transferred into Paradise*, in which are Enoch and Elijah. And in this way they will be *preserved unharmed from the persecution of Antichrist*. And that then Enoch and Elijah themselves would descend on the earth for the purpose of preaching [against] Antichrist. Then they would be killed by him or by his servants, and thus *Antichrist would reign for a long time*. But when the Antichrist is dead, Dolcino himself, who then would be the holy pope, and his preserved followers, will descend on the earth, and will preach the right faith of Christ to all, and will convert those who will be living then to the true faith of Jesus Christ."[37]

Several points in this remarkable statement bear close similarity to modern pre-Tribulationism.

1. The Latin word *transferrentur*, meaning "they would be transferred," is the same word used by medieval

     Christians to describe the rapture of Enoch to heaven.

2. The subjects of this rapture were to be Brother Dolcino and his followers. This was not a partial Rapture theory, because Brother Dolcino considered the Apostolic Brethren to be the true church in contrast to the Roman Catholic Church.

3. The purpose of the Rapture was to preserve the people from the persecution of the Antichrist.

4. The text presents the "transference" of believers to heaven and the "descent" of believers from heaven as two separate events.

5. The text also shows that quite a long gap of time must intervene between the rapture of the saints to heaven and the return of the saints from heaven.[38]

Francis Gumerlock, an expert on the Brother Dolcino text, clearly believes that this is a pre-Tribulation Rapture statement. He concludes:

> This paragraph from *The History of Brother Dolcino* indicates that in northern Italy in the early fourteenth century a teaching very similar to modern pre-Tribulationalism was being preached. Responding to distressing political and ecclesiastical conditions, Dolcino engaged in detailed speculations about eschatology and believed that the coming of the Antichrist was imminent. He also believed that the means by which God would protect His people from the persecution of the Antichrist would be through a translation of the saints to paradise.[39]

These two ancient witnesses are enough to show that the pre-Tribulationist view isn't a recent invention, but there's one more that's much closer to home.

Ivy League

One of the clearest references to a pre-Tribulation Rapture view being held before the time of J. N. Darby came from a Baptist named Morgan Edwards. Founder of the Ivy League's Brown University, Edwards saw a distinct Rapture three and a half years before the start of the Millennium. The teaching of Edwards, who wrote about his pre-Tribulationist beliefs in 1744 and later published them in 1788, is significant.

He taught the following about the Rapture:

> *The distance between the first and second resurrection will be somewhat more than a thousand years.*
>
> I say, *somewhat more—*, because the dead saints will be raised, and the living changed at Christ's "appearing in the air" (I Thes. Iv. 17); and this will be about three years and a half before the *millennium,* as we shall see hereafter: but will he and they abide in the air all that time? No: they will ascend to paradise, or to some one of those many "mansions in the father's house" (John xiv. 2), and disappear during the foresaid period of time. The design of this retreat and disappearing will be to judge the risen and changed saints; for "now the time is come that judgment must begin," and that will be "at the house of God" (I Pet. Iv. 17).[40]

Notice that Edwards makes three essential points consistent with the pre-Tribulationist view: (1) He clearly separates the

Rapture from the Second Coming by three and a half years. (2) He uses modern pre-Tribulation Rapture verses (see 1 Thessalonians 4:17 and John 14:2) to describe the Rapture and support his view. (3) He believed that the judgment seat of Christ (rewarding) for believers will occur in heaven while the Tribulation rages on earth.

The only difference between modern pre-Tribulationism and Edwards' belief is the time interval of three and a half years, instead of seven, between the Rapture and the Second Coming. This, however, does not mean that Edwards was a mid-Tribulationist, since it appears that he believed that the total length of the Tribulation was to be three and a half years.[41]

The idea that the pre-Tribulation Rapture is a recent invention is a well-worn "straw man" argument. It's simply not historically accurate. A person may choose to reject the pre-Tribulationist position, but no rejection of this view should be based on this faulty argument.

Question #2: Can Those Who Hear and Reject the Gospel Before the Rapture Be Saved During the Tribulation?

Almost all students of end-time prophecy would agree that people will be saved during the Tribulation period. In fact, the salvation of lost men and women is one of the chief purposes of the Tribulation period.

Speaking of these dark days, the prophet Joel wrote, "And anyone who calls on the name of the LORD will be saved. There will be people on Mount Zion in Jerusalem who escape, just as the LORD has said. These will be among the survivors whom the Lord has called" (2:32, NLT).

Revelation 7:9–14 indicates that there will be great revival during the Great Tribulation. Even so, many respected students of Bible prophecy contend that anyone who hears the gospel before the Rapture, understands it, and then openly rejects it will be precluded by God from ever being saved during the Tribulation. They hold that God will send strong deception upon those who heard the truth and rejected God's offer of mercy before the Rapture. Support for this view is usually based on 2 Thessalonians 2:9–12:

> That is, the one whose coming is in accord with the activity of Satan, with all power and signs and false wonders, and with all the deception of wickedness for those who perish, because they did not receive the love of the truth so as to be saved. For this reason God will send upon them a deluding influence so that they will believe what is false, in order that they all may be judged who did not believe the truth, but took pleasure in wickedness.

While this verse could be used to support such a position, it does not seem to refer to people who reject the truth before the Rapture, but rather those who reject the truth and receive the Antichrist *after* the Rapture. The context of this entire passage describes what happens during the Tribulation period and refers to those who witness the deception of Antichrist, believe his message, and reject the truth. According to this passage, God will condemn such people. He will confirm them in their unbelief and send strong delusion on them so that they will believe the lie.

I believe that many who have rejected the gospel before the Rapture will roll along the same railroad tracks after the

Rapture and reject it again. To say, based on this verse, however, that no one who has clearly heard the claims of Christ before the Rapture and rejected them can receive God's mercy during the Tribulation makes this verse say much more than the context allows.

God will use the horror of the Tribulation period to bring millions of sinners to faith in His Son (see Revelation 7:9–14). Among this numberless multitude there will certainly be some who previously rejected the Lord before the Rapture but will admit their error and humbly accept Jesus Christ as the Son of God who purchased a pardon from sin for them on the cross.

What a gracious Savior!

Question #3: What Will Happen to Babies and Young Children at the Rapture?

As you might imagine, parents with small children ask this question frequently. Believing parents want to know if their young children who have not yet trusted Christ will be left behind when Christ comes for His church.

It's important at the outset to note that there are no specific Scriptures that address this question. Nevertheless, there are three main views on this issue.

View #1: No Children Will Be Included in the Rapture

Those who hold this view emphasize that the Rapture is only for believers and that if a person has not personally believed in Christ, he or she is not eligible for the Rapture. They would point out that in the flood and destruction of the inhabitants of Canaan, small children were not excluded from the judgment.

View #2: All Infants and Young Children Will Be Raptured to Heaven Before the Tribulation

Adherents of this view are quick to point out the Scripture's strong implication that children who die young have a place in heaven. Several passages in the Bible, including 2 Samuel 12:20–23, Matthew 19:13–15, and Mark 10:13–16, seem to support this position. Since all young children or infants who have never put saving faith in Christ go to heaven when they die, many would argue that they will also go to heaven in the Rapture and be exempted from the horrors of the Tribulation. This is the view that is presented in the Left Behind series by LaHaye and Jenkins. In this series, all children under the age of twelve are raptured, regardless of the spiritual condition of their parents.

While I agree that infants and small children who die go to heaven to be with Christ, I do not believe that this necessarily means that they will participate in the Rapture. These are two different issues.

View #3: Infants and Young Children of Believers Will Be Raptured to Heaven Before the Tribulation

This is a mediating view between views 1 and 2. While one should avoid dogmatism on this issue, I believe that this is the best view for two reasons. First, Paul reminds us in 1 Corinthians 7:14 that in a Christian family the children are "set apart for Him." It seems inconceivable to me that the Lord would rapture believing parents to heaven and leave their defenseless children alone in the world for the Tribulation period.

Second, I believe that there is biblical precedent for this view. When the Lord sent the flood on the earth during the days of Noah, all the world was destroyed, including unbelieving men, women, and children. But God delivered Noah, his wife, and his three sons and their wives. Likewise, when God

destroyed Sodom and Gomorrah he destroyed all the inhabitants of the cities including the children of unbelievers. The
only ones to escape were Lot and his two daughters. Also, in
Egypt at the first Passover the homes of believers, including
their young children, were protected from the judgment of
God by the blood of the lamb on the doorpost. In each of these
cases the believer and his children were delivered from the time
of judgment, while unbelievers and their children were not.

While I recognize that Noah's three sons and Lot's daughters
were not infants or small children and were probably believers
themselves, I believe that these incidents provide a strong biblical precedent. When God sends cataclysmic judgment He
rescues both the believer and his children but allows unbelievers
and their children to face judgment.

I believe that the young children of unbelievers will have the
opportunity to believe in Christ as they come of age during the
Tribulation period. Those who die during the Tribulation before
they are old enough to understand the claims of the gospel will
be taken to heaven to be with Christ.

Finally, regardless of which view one holds, the one fact that
we can all rest in is that God is a God of love, compassion, mercy,
and justice. Whatever He does when the Rapture occurs will be
wise, righteous, and fair. God loves our children more than we
do. Indeed, they are "precious in His sight."

Question #4: If All Believers Are Raptured *Before* the Tribulation, Who Are the Believers on Earth *During* the Tribulation?

Matthew 24:31 says that, at the end of the Tribulation, when
Jesus returns from heaven to earth at His glorious second com-

ing, "He will send forth His angels with a great trumpet and they will gather together His elect from the four winds, from one end of the sky to the other."

This raises a very important question: If all believers are caught up to heaven before the Tribulation begins, who are these believers ("the elect") on earth during the Tribulation?

Of course, post-Tribulationists say that these "elect" are the church on earth who have survived the Tribulation. Pre-Tribulationists, on the other hand, hold that these are people—Jewish believers, in the context of Matthew 24—who will be saved during the horrendous days of God's judgment and wrath. These people who come to Christ after the Rapture and during the Tribulation are often referred to as "Tribulation believers" or "Tribulation saints."

Revelation 7 presents two groups of Tribulation believers: 144,000 Jewish believers (twelve thousand from each of the twelve tribes of Israel, see vv. 1–8) and a numberless host who will be martyred for their faith (see vv. 9–14).

Another related question that always comes up is how these people will come to faith during the Tribulation if all the believers have been removed. Who will share the gospel message with them?

The Bible doesn't tell us for certain, but it may be that the 144,000 Jews each has a personal "Saul of Tarsus Damascus Road experience." Dramatically saved, they will be "set on fire" and spread the gospel message around the globe.

No doubt many will be saved by reading their Bibles, listening to tapes of sermons, watching Christian DVDs, or reading Christian books, especially ones about the end times (maybe even this book). Surely, many people will be searching for answers in the aftermath of the Rapture. Many others may be brought to faith in Christ simply by remembering the truth of the gospel that someone shared with them before the Rapture.

This should motivate us to plant the seeds of the gospel wherever we can. We never know when God may water the seeds and bring them to life.

I have to admit that we don't know for sure what means God will use to save people during the Tribulation. But we know for certain that it will happen. Jesus said that by the end of the Tribulation, "this gospel of the kingdom shall be preached in the whole world as a testimony to all the nations, and then the end will come" (Matthew 24:14).

May God help us to faithfully spread His message while there's still time.

Question #5: If Believers Will Be Raptured to Heaven Before the Tribulation, Why Does the Bible Tell Us So Much About Those Years?

As we have already seen, the Bible contains a great deal of very specific information about the seven-year Tribulation. Large sections from the Old Testament prophets graphically portray the coming Day of the Lord. Revelation devotes fourteen full chapters to those years.

But this raises a very good question: If God raptures believers before He unleashes the years of Tribulation, why does He give us so much information about it?

Even though I believe that all true believers will be raptured to heaven before the Tribulation and escape God's wrath, it's still important for us to know about the key players and events of this seven-year period. There are at least three major reasons why God gave us this information and why we should inform ourselves about the Tribulation.

Truths from the Tribulation

First, what God has revealed to us about the Tribulation is like a final crash course in theology. From Genesis to Jude, the Lord unveils great theological truths about Himself, man, creation, salvation, the church, angels, Satan and demons, and the end times. In many places in the Bible—but especially in Revelation 6–18—God gives us a final, condensed crash course on theology by presenting to us the conditions of the final years of this age.

What are some of the great truths that we learn from the Tribulation? These seven fateful years teach us a great deal about the nature of man, God, and Satan.

- We learn (if we hadn't realized it already) that man is sinful, easily deceived, and rebellious.
- We learn that God is holy and that He unleashes His wrath against sin.
- We're also reminded that He is gracious and will save millions of people, even in earth's darkest hour (see Revelation 7:9–14).

The Tribulation also unmasks Satan. Timothy Demy and Thomas Ice note,

> The tribulation is important because, in a sense, Satan is unmasked and we see his ultimate intentions and purposes. Such an understanding of his plan, if properly applied, can aid the believer today in spiritual warfare.
>
> For example, we note that during the tribulation, Satan uses religion in a false and deceptive way. This stands as a warning for us today.[42]

Studying the Tribulation gives us insight for living today.

Warning: Danger Ahead

Second, the Tribulation serves as a sobering warning sign for every generation of the consequences of man's sin. John MacArthur makes this point very clearly:

> Some have asked why the Lord would warn people during the New Testament times as He does in this message, when He knew they would never live to experience these terrible signs. Indeed, why include this in the Gospel account, where it has stood as a warning to the church in every generation? But a similar question could be asked about Isaiah's prophecy and his warnings about the Babylonian captivity (Isaiah 39:6–7), which did not occur until after all the people in Isaiah's generation were dead. The message is given to be a warning to all about the consequences of sin—and it will stand as a specific warning to those who will actually experience the terrible judgment.[43]

Friends of God

Third, even though we won't experience the Tribulation if we know the Savior, the Lord loves to take His own people into His confidence and tell us what is going to happen even if it doesn't directly affect our own lives.

Remember Genesis 18. God came to Abraham and told him that He was going to destroy the wicked cities of Sodom and Gomorrah. This had no immediate impact on Abraham. He didn't live in these cities. He wasn't going to be there when God's judgment fell. But God told Abraham about it anyway. Why?

Because Abraham was the friend of God (see 2 Chronicles 20:7; James 2:23).

The Lord said to Abraham, "Shall I hide from Abraham what I am about to do, since Abraham will surely become a great and mighty nation, and in him all the nations of the earth will be blessed? For I have chosen him" (Genesis 18:17–19). This revelation led Abraham to plead for God's mercy and the salvation of those in the doomed cities.

Like Abraham, even though we won't be here during the Tribulation, God has graciously taken us into His confidence and shown us what He will do on earth during the final dark days of this age. Jesus said that we too are His friends (see Luke 12:4; John 15:14–15). And, like Abraham, having received the revelation of what's ahead, we should be moved to pray for those who are still under the wrath of God.

What a privilege it is to know the mind of God and His prophetic program for the final seven years of this present age!

Question #6: Doesn't the Pre-Tribulation Rapture Give People False Hope?

A common allegation against the pre-Tribulationist view is that we are giving people false hope that they will escape the coming years of suffering and judgment. It is alleged that we are telling pampered Christians what they want to hear and setting them up for a massive disappointment when it turns out to be untrue.

Pre-Tribbers are accused of sowing the seeds of potential disillusionment. Rather than offering false hope, these detractors contend, we should be preparing believers for the Tribulation, and the failure to do so will leave them totally unprepared and unable to endure the suffering of those years.

The argument goes like this: If the pre-Tribulation Rapture turns out to be untrue, there will be millions of self-indulgent, materialistic believers who will be totally disillusioned if they are expecting the Rapture before the Tribulation and will then wake up one day to find the teaching that they had received to be terribly wrong. I've even heard people go so far as to say that when it turns out that believers really will be around for the Tribulation, they will turn on the pastors and teachers who falsely misled them into believing that they would escape.

There are four problems with this view. First, this question assumes up front that the pre-Tribulationist position is incorrect—quite a major assumption in light of what we've already seen in this book! An argument such as this one—railing against the pre-Tribulationist view—is based more on emotion and fear than on sound biblical interpretation.

Second, even if the pre-Tribulationist view is wrong, are God's Spirit-indwelled people so weak, shallow, and defenseless that we would all crumble under the pressure just because our biblical interpretation turned out to be faulty? What a cynical, pessimistic view! It minimizes the sustaining, energizing power of the Holy Spirit in the life of the believer.

Third, let's assume that one does believe that Christians will face the Tribulation. What should he do to get ready for it? Revisit all of those Y2K fears? Build a compound out in the wilderness? Take a course on survival skills? Store up enough food for seven years? Gather a stockpile of weapons? Bury a coffee can of gold coins in the backyard? Go to church more? Memorize more Bible verses? Where does it stop? Those who argue that the pre-Tribulationist view will leave people unprepared for the Tribulation usually don't do anything to get people ready for the Tribulation, either. It's just rhetoric.

For that matter, the Bible itself never gives us any specific details for how to prepare for the Tribulation. To me, that's a strong argument that we won't be here during that time.

Fourth, the Bible indicates that a host of people will be saved on earth after the Rapture, including millions who will be martyred for their faith in Christ (see Revelation 7:9–14). If these brand-new baby believers are able to trust in the Lord even in the face of martyrdom, why would we doubt God's sufficiency to help the rest of us make it through?[44]

Having exposed the fallacies behind this question, let me make it clear that I don't believe that we are headed for any disillusionment or disappointment. Our blessed hope is that Jesus will catch us up and deliver us from the wrath to come, just as He promised.

Question #7: Is It Ever Right to Set a Date for the Rapture?

I read one time about a man who, while giving a lecture, said, "I calculate that the Rapture will come in 217 million years."

Someone in the audience, greatly agitated, interrupted the speaker. "How many years did you say?"

"Two hundred seventeen million," the teacher repeated.

The hearer, sitting down in great relief, said, "Oh, man, you frightened me. I thought you said *one* hundred seventeen million!"

The following personal ad appeared in a newspaper: "Yesterday in this space I predicted that the world would come to an end. It did not, however. I regret any inconvenience this may have caused."

Setting specific dates for events in the end times does more than cause inconvenience. It's not just an amusing game of "name that date" that we can all laugh at when it proves to be wrong. Why? Because when the predicted date comes and goes (which always happens), people can use this failed calculation as further fuel to discredit the Bible and lead others to become more disillusioned with its teachings.

Nevertheless, this hasn't stopped people from giving it their best try. Ever since the early days of the church, people have tried to calculate the time of Christ's coming. There seems to be an almost irresistible attraction for some people to try to name the year, month, or even exact day of the Rapture. Date-setting appears to be almost a form of spiritual "hobby" for them.

Date-Setters' Hall of Shame

A website called the Library of Date Setters chronicles two hundred known predictions of the Rapture or the end of the world.[45] This website serves as a kind of hall of fame (or shame) of date-setting. Here are just a few of the more significant ones:

Person Making the Prediction	Date the Rapture Was to Occur
Hippolytus (c. AD 200) and Lactantius	AD 500 (c. AD 300)
A host of people caught up in the hysteria of the new millennium	AD 1000
William Miller (Baptist pastor in Vermont who gave rise to the Adventist tradition)	1843–1844
Charles Taze Russell (Jehovah's Witness)	1910 (Rapture), 1914 (end of the world)

Edgar C. Whisenant (wrote a book titled *88 Reasons Why the Rapture Will Be in 1988.* The book isn't selling too well these days. He wrote another book in 1989, *89 Reasons Why the Rapture Will Be in 1989,* and it didn't sell nearly as well as the first one!	September 11–13, 1988
Harold Camping (wrote a book titled *Are You Ready?*)	September 1994

Since I have written several books on end-time prophecy, people frequently send me their predictions for the date of the Rapture. In the spring of 2003 I received a letter from a man who told me that he had correctly calculated the time of the Rapture. His letter was filled with all kinds of dates, disconnected facts, unfounded assumptions, and complicated calculations. But at the end of all this, *voila!,* he had computed the exact day of the Rapture.

His conclusion, based on all his decipherings, was that the Rapture was coming on Nisan 17, 2003, or April 19. The interesting thing is that the letter was sent to me via another ministry that I sometimes help, so I didn't receive the letter until April 22—*three days after* the Rapture was supposed to have occurred.

Date-setting is folly! The sad thing is that humiliation or lack of success doesn't seem to deter many would-be prophetic authorities. Their motto seems to be "Why not keep guessing? In this game you only have to be right once."

Date-Setters Beware

Make no mistake. The Bible strictly prohibits date-setting for the coming of Christ. All who engage in date-setting need to hear these words from the lips of Jesus Himself:

Therefore be on the alert, for you do not know which day your Lord is coming. (Matthew 24:42)

For this reason you also must be ready; for the Son of Man is coming at an hour when you do not think He will. (Matthew 24:44)

Be on the alert then, for you do not know the day nor the hour. (Matthew 25:13)

He said to them, "It is not for you to know times or epochs which the Father has fixed by His own authority." (Acts 1:7)

It's interesting to me that the book of Revelation—by far our most complete source of information about the last days—never mentions any specific date for Christ's coming or any other event. All God tells us in the last book of the Bible about the timing of His coming is that it will occur quickly (see Revelation 1:1, 3; 3:11; 22:7, 12, 20).

Incredibly, in spite of the clear teaching of Scripture, people continue to set dates for the coming of Christ. Jesus claimed that during His earthly ministry even *He* did not know the day of His coming. "'But of that day and hour no one knows, not even the angels of heaven, nor the Son, but the Father alone'" (Matthew 24:36). Now, however, seated at the right hand of the Majesty on high, I have no doubt that He knows that day—and hour and second and millisecond.

Anyone who purports to know the specific time of Christ's coming is claiming that he knows something that the Father didn't even tell the Son while He was on earth! This is the height of arrogance and folly.

Imminency and Date-Setting—Like Oil and Water

The truth of the imminent coming of Christ shows date-setting for the Rapture to be the misguided, illegitimate activity that it really is. Just think about it. Whenever someone sets such a date, it's tantamount to a declaration that Jesus Christ cannot return at any moment. For instance, if someone today were to announce his firm calculation that the Rapture will occur on September 10, 2020, then by doing so he is flatly saying that Christ *can't* come before that time, wiping out any notion of His imminent return for His own. And since the Bible clearly teaches the imminent return of Jesus, date-setting is never legitimate.

This is another reason for us to reject any form of precise prediction for the timing of the Rapture. It takes the form of another commonly asked question:

Question #8: Will Believers Who Have Been Raptured to Heaven Be Able to Watch the Events of the Tribulation Unfold on Earth?

We've probably all asked this question at one time or another. How much will we see? How much will we know when we're on the other side?

The main passage used to support the idea that departed believers in heaven are watching the events on earth is Hebrews 12:1. Following the inspiring list of the faithful from the past such as Enoch, Abraham, and Moses, the writer to the Hebrews concludes, *"Therefore, since we have so great a cloud of witnesses surrounding us..."* (italics added). You may have heard this huge cloud of witnesses described as an audience in a heavenly stadium watching us here on earth.

But I believe in this particular passage the writer's emphasis is not that we ought to be motivated because they see us, but rather because we see them! As we look back on the patient endurance and faithfulness in the lives of the saints of old, they are witnesses that should motivate us to emulate their lives.

The Bible does reveal that when we get to heaven we will be aware of at least some events that are transpiring on the earth. Samuel the prophet, after his death, appeared to King Saul and was aware of at least some of the events surrounding Saul and his kingdom (see 1 Samuel 28:16–18). The rejoicing in heaven over the salvation of a sinner on earth seems to include believers who are already in heaven as well as angels (see Luke 15:7, 10).

The martyrs in heaven in Revelation 6:9–10 are aware that their persecutors are still alive on earth during the Tribulation. Also, the multitude in heaven in Revelation 19:1–6 is aware of the destruction of Babylon on earth near the end of the Tribulation.

Whether God will limit our knowledge of events on earth or allow us to know everything that transpires is not specifically stated. What can be scripturally stated is that those who are in heaven know at least *some* of what is happening on this earth and follow those events with intense interest.

Then again, once we get to heaven, we may not be as interested in watching the events on earth as we might think. Revelation 4–5 depicts the twenty-four elders—representative of the church—worshiping the Lord during the Tribulation. While we will more than likely know at least some of the main events that are occurring on earth during those seven years of judgment, it's clear from Revelation that when we get to heaven we will primarily be consumed with worshiping the Lamb on the throne, not watching the Tribulation on earth.

Question #9: Are There Any More Prophecies That Must Be Fulfilled Before the Rapture Can Occur?

Prophecy teachers will often point out that "there are no more prophecies that must be fulfilled for the Rapture to occur."

True enough. But this is also somewhat misleading.

What the statement implies is that there *were* some signs that had to be fulfilled first, but now there are none. Scripture, however, teaches that there are no signs that must take place before Jesus appears in the clouds and calls us home. The Rapture is a signless, imminent, any-moment event from the human point of view. None of the key passages in the New Testament mentions any signs that must occur before the Rapture. All that has to happen in order for Jesus to come is for Jesus to come.

All the signs listed in Scripture—in Daniel, the Olivet Discourse (see Matthew 24), and Revelation—relate to the second coming of Christ to earth, not the Rapture. This is a very important distinction to understand.

As we see the prophetic highway markers in Scripture lining up, one after another, we must remember that these signs denote the approaching Tribulation and second coming of Christ to establish His kingdom. And you know what that means. If those events are coming soon, the Rapture will be even sooner!

Question #10: How Will People Who Are Left Behind Explain the Rapture?

The Rapture will be the most amazing event in the history of the world. In a split second of time millions of people will disappear from this earth without a trace (except, perhaps, for a pile of clothes). One has to wonder—how in the world will the people who are left behind explain this unparalleled event? The world will be left in a total chaos of unmanned cars, pilotless planes, teacherless classrooms, and workerless factories. Missing persons reports will jam phone lines around the world. How will people explain it?

There will undoubtedly be two main categories of explanation: a natural one and a supernatural one. The natural explanations will be the most popular, as the pundits flood the airwaves with their theories. TV talks shows and cable news channels will have numerous guests debating their viewpoints. Conspiracy theories will abound. *Nightline* will have a two-week special to investigate the possible explanations.

Who knows what kind of bizarre ideas will be presented? A massive UFO abduction? A time warp? A new weapon of mass destruction? People will be at a loss to explain the Rapture, but that won't stop them from trying!

The other explanation for the Rapture will be the supernatural explanation. Many people who have been left behind will suddenly remember a conversation with a believer about the end times. Unsaved church members will remember sermons that they had mostly dismissed at the time. The Rapture may be one of the greatest evangelistic events of all time as millions of people who have heard about the Rapture but never received Christ suddenly realize that they've been left behind.

While the so-called experts concoct their theories, thousands of people will realize what has happened and will humbly bow the knee to Christ. These "Tribulation saints" will be persecuted and even martyred for their faith (see Revelation 6:9; 7:13–14; 20:4). But when they leave this earth they will join the mighty company of the redeemed around the throne to worship the Lamb.

THE TEACHING
OF THE RAPTURE
FOR TODAY

My prayer is that the Lord will use this book to help you see that Jesus could come today—to help you believe in the imminent, any-moment coming of Christ for His bride. But I want this book to do more than just convince you of the truth and timing of the Rapture. Much more.

If we truly believe these things, it's bound to have a dramatic impact on the way that we live out our lives every day. It's one thing to talk about the Rapture and the "sweet bye and bye," but we all have to live each day in the "nasty now and now." Belief in the any-moment Rapture should empower our daily lives as we face the trials, struggles, and joys of life. Knowing my future should deeply impact my present.

In this final section of the book I want to focus on the impact that the any-moment Rapture should have on our daily lives, how it should change the way that we live each day as we await His coming.

14

PRE-TRIB AND PREPARED!

Several years ago during a question-and-answer session at a prophecy conference I heard one of the speakers say, "I believe in the three P's of Bible prophecy. I'm premillennial, pre-Trib, and prepared."

I like that.

That's really the key. Now, don't get me wrong. What we believe is very important, and we should never minimize it. I wrote this book to present what I believe that the Bible teaches us about the rapture of the church. If it doesn't matter, then I've wasted my time and yours.

God spent a great deal of time and ink telling us what to expect in the future. It's vital to know these things. But while it's important what doctrines we hold, it's equally important what doctrines hold us. What real, practical, and observable difference do these truths make in our lives each day?

Every major New Testament passage on the Rapture contains a practical application that is closely associated with it. Prophecy was not given just to stir our imagination or capture our attention. Prophecy is intended by God to change our attitudes and actions to be more in line with His Word and His character.

Prophecy scholar Charles Dyer emphasizes this transforming purpose:

> "God gave prophecy to change our hearts, not to fill our heads with knowledge. God never predicted future events just to satisfy our curiosity about the future. Every time God announces events that are future, He includes with His predictions practical applications to life. God's pronouncements about the future carry with them specific advice for the 'here and now.'"[46]

According to the Bible, there are at least seven life-changing effects or influences that understanding the Rapture should have on our hearts. Let's consider these as we draw this book to a conclusion.

The Rapture Has a Converting Influence on Seeking Hearts

No person knows how much time he or she has left on this earth, either personally or prophetically. Personally, most of us are painfully aware of our mortality. We have no guarantee that we will see tomorrow. Prophetically, Christ could come at any moment to take His bride, the church, to heaven, and all unbelievers will be left behind to endure the horrors of the Tribulation period.

With this in mind, the most important question for every reader to face is whether or not he or she has a personal relationship with Jesus Christ as Savior. The message of salvation through Jesus Christ is a message that contains both bad news and good news.

The bad news is that the Bible declares that all people, including you and me, are sinful and therefore separated from the Holy God of the universe (see Isaiah 59:2; Romans 3:23). God is holy and cannot simply overlook or wink at sin. A just payment for the debt must be made. But we are spiritually bankrupt and have no resources within ourselves to pay the huge debt that we owe.

The Good News, or gospel, is that Jesus Christ has come and satisfied our sin debt. He bore our judgment and paid the price for our sins. He died on the cross for our sins and was raised to life on the third day to prove conclusively that the work of salvation had been fully accomplished. Colossians 2:14 says, "Having canceled out the certificate of debt consisting of decrees against us, which was hostile to us; and He has taken it out of the way, having nailed it to the cross." First Peter 3:18 says, "For Christ also died for sins once for all, the just for the unjust, so that He might bring us to God."

The salvation that Christ accomplished for us is available to all through faith in Jesus Christ. Salvation from sin is a free gift that God offers to sinful people who deserve judgment. Won't you receive the gift today? Place your faith and trust in Christ, and in Him alone, for your eternal salvation. "Believe in the Lord Jesus, and you will be saved" (Acts 16:31).

Now that you know the truth of the Rapture and that those who fail to trust Christ will be left behind to endure the Tribulation, won't you respond to the invitation before it's too late?

Accept Christ personally by calling upon Him to save you from you sins. You can do it right now, right where you are. Make sure that you're Rapture ready!

The Rapture Has a Caring Influence on Soul-Winning Hearts

No believer in Jesus Christ can study Bible prophecy without being gripped by the awesome power and wrath of God. Understanding the looming end-time events brings us face to face with what's at stake for those who don't know Christ as their Savior. We are reminded in 2 Corinthians 5:20 of our calling during this present age. "Therefore, we are ambassadors for Christ, as though God were making an appeal through us; we beg you on behalf of Christ, be reconciled to God." Those who have already responded to the message of God's grace and forgiveness through Christ know where this planet is headed, and we are Christ's ambassadors representing Him and His interests to a perishing world.

The Rapture Has a Cleansing Influence on Sinning Hearts

The Word of God clearly teaches that a proper understanding of the Rapture should produce a life of holiness and purity. "Beloved, now we are children of God, and it has not appeared as yet what we will be. We know that when He appears, we will be like Him, because we will see Him just as He is. And everyone who has this hope fixed on Him purifies himself, just as He is pure" (1 John 3:2–3). Focusing the mind and heart on prophecy, especially on Christ's coming, is a fail-safe formula for maintaining personal purity. Note the certainty: "And all who believe this *will* keep themselves pure."

Here then is a perfect prescription for living a life of holiness: focusing on the literal reality of the Rapture and our sudden translation from this planet into His very presence in the clouds of heaven.

As I already mentioned briefly in chapter 19, a book was published in 1988 entitled *88 Reasons Why Christ Will Return in 1988*. In the book the author stated that he had conclusive proof that Christ would rapture the Church to heaven in September 1988. A friend of mine who was a pastor in eastern Oklahoma called me in the summer of 1988 to ask me some questions about the book. In our conversation he told me that the book had caused quite a furor among many people in his church and other churches in the area. Of course, the Bible clearly declares that date-setting concerning the coming of Christ is futile and foolish (see Matthew 24:36; Luke 21:8). This erroneous book, however, caused many people to reexamine their lives—just in case the author was right! Even though this book was totally incorrect, it did have the effect of causing some people to reexamine their lives in the light of Christ's soon return.

The question is, What happened to those same people in *October* of 1988? Did they stay faithful, glancing now and again at the sky as they anticipated the coming of Jesus? The fact is that the Bible declares that we are *always* to be looking for Christ's coming, not just when someone sets an arbitrary date. "Live sensibly, righteously and godly in the present age, looking for the blessed hope and the appearing of the glory of our great God and Savior, Christ Jesus" (Titus 2:12–13).

Prophecy and purity are mentioned together in Romans 13:11–14:

Another reason for right living is that you know how late it is; time is running out. Wake up, for the coming of our salvation is nearer now than when we first believed. The night is almost gone; the day of salvation will soon be here. So don't live in darkness. Get rid of your evil deeds. Shed them like dirty clothes. Clothe yourselves with the armor of right living, as those who live in the light. We should be decent and true in everything we do, so that everyone can approve of our behavior. Don't participate in wild parties and getting drunk, or in adultery and immoral living, or in fighting and jealously. But let the Lord Jesus Christ take control of you, and don't think of ways to indulge your evil desires. (NLT)

The practical, cleansing effect of prophecy is also presented in 2 Peter 3:10–14:

But the day of the Lord will come like a thief, in which the heavens will pass away with a roar and the elements will be destroyed with intense heat, and the earth and its works will be burned up. Since all these things are to be destroyed in this way, what sort of people ought you to be in holy conduct and godliness, looking for and hastening the coming of the day of God, because of which the heavens will be destroyed by burning, and the elements will melt with intense heat! But according to His promise we are looking for new heavens and a new earth, in which righteousness dwells. Therefore, beloved, since you look for these things, be diligent to be found by Him in peace, spotless and blameless.

When anyone makes the comment that studying Bible prophecy isn't practical, he or she is revealing a lack of understanding about the powerful personal impact of considering these truths. In an immoral, sinful society like ours, what could be more practical than personal purity?

The Rapture Has a Calming Influence on Stirred Hearts

Another practical effect of the Rapture is that it has a calming influence on us when we find our hearts stirred up and troubled. In John 14:1–3 Jesus said, "Do not let your heart be troubled; believe in God, believe also in Me. In my Father's house are many dwelling places; if it were not so, I would have told you; for I go to prepare a place for you. If I go and prepare a place for you, I will come again and receive you to Myself, that where I am, there you may be also."

The word *troubled* means "to be stirred up, disturbed, unsettled, or thrown into confusion." There are many things in our world today to disturb and unsettle us: the moral decay in our society, crime, economic uncertainty, terrorism, and racial unrest, just to cite a few. All of these worries, of course, are added on top of the personal problems, struggles, and difficulties that we all face in our daily lives. Trouble is the common denominator of all mankind. And often these hardships, perplexities, and sorrows can leave us distraught, distracted, and disturbed. One of the great comforts in times like these is remembering that our Lord will someday return to take us to be with Himself.

In John 14:1–3, our Lord emphasizes three main points to calm our troubled hearts: a person, a place, and a promise. The person is Jesus Himself, the place is the heavenly city (New Jerusalem), and the promise is that He will come again to take us to be with Him forever.

The Rapture Has a Comforting Influence on Sorrowing Hearts

Every person reading these words has either faced or will face the grief of losing a close friend or loved one in death. When death strikes, pious platitudes do little to bring lasting comfort to friends and family. The only real, enduring comfort when death takes someone we love is the hope that we will see that person again in heaven. God's Word tells us with certainty that we are not to sorrow as people who have no hope, because we will be reunited with our saved loved ones and friends at the Rapture:

> But we do not want you to be uninformed, brethren, about those who are asleep, so that you will not grieve as do the rest who have no hope. For if we believe that Jesus died and rose again, even so God will bring with Him those who have fallen asleep in Jesus. For this we say to you by the word of the Lord, that we who are alive and remain until the coming of the Lord, will not precede those who have fallen asleep. For the Lord Himself will descend from heaven with a shout, with the voice of the archangel and with the trumpet of God, and the dead in Christ will rise first. Then we who are alive and remain will be caught up together with them in the clouds to meet the Lord in the air, and so we shall always be with the Lord. Therefore comfort one another with these words. (1 Thessalonians 4:13–18)

The truth of the Rapture should transform the way that we view death. God has promised that death has lost its sting, that it will ultimately be abolished, and that life will reign. This is not to say that we shouldn't grieve when our friends or loved ones die. Jesus wept at the tomb of Lazarus (see John 11:35). Stephen's friends wept loudly over his battered body (see Acts 8:2). The Bible declares, however, that our weeping is not the weeping of despair. Our Savior wants us to find deep solace, hope, and comfort for our sorrowing hearts in the truth of God's Word about the future for His children.

The Rapture Has a Controlling Influence on Serving Hearts

In 1 Corinthians 15:58, after presenting the truth of the Rapture, Paul concludes with a strong admonition: "Therefore, my beloved brethren, be steadfast, immovable, always abounding in the work of the Lord, knowing that your toil is not in vain in the Lord."

Since you *know* that Christ will someday come to receive you to Himself, Paul tells us, let nothing move you; be strong and steady in your Christian service. So many today are unstable and unsettled in Christian work. They are constantly vacillating. Knowing about Christ's coming and future events should cure the problem of instability and inconsistency in Christian labor. Realizing and meditating on the fact that Christ could return at any time will make us more enthusiastic, energetic, and excited about serving the Lord.

The first two questions that Saul, who later became Paul, asked when he saw the glorified Christ on the road to Damascus were "Who are You, Lord?" and "What shall I do?" (Acts 22:8, 10). Many professing Christians today have never been past the first question. Many believers in Christ are spiritually unemployed!

The principle in the Bible is clear: waiters are workers. When Christ comes we are to "be dressed for service and well prepared" (Luke 12:35, NLT). If the Rapture is a reality to us, it will motivate us to work faithfully for our Lord. The Lord intends for our knowledge of Bible prophecy to translate into devoted service for those around us as we await His return.

Warren Wiersbe tells a story of when he was a young man preaching on the last days, with all the events of prophecy clearly laid out and perfectly planned. At the end of the service an older gentleman came up to him and whispered in his ear, "I used to have the Lord's return planned out to the last detail, but years ago I moved from the planning committee to the welcoming committee."

Certainly we want to study Bible prophecy and know about God's plan for the future. That's what this book is all about. But we must be careful not to get too caught up in the planning and forget the welcoming. Are you on the welcoming committee for the Lord's coming? Are you living each day to please the Master?

May God help this study of the Rapture to transform our lives as we eagerly wait for our Savior to come.

The Rapture Has a Clarifying Influence on Searching Hearts

I once read about a man talking to a friend about his preacher. He said, "My pastor is the best man I know at taking the Bible apart, but the only problem is that he can't put it back together again." Many Christians have this same problem to one degree or another.

Twenty-eight percent of the Bible was prophecy at the time that it was written. We can't really understand the Bible without understanding at least the basics of prophecy. And the Rapture is a central cog in God's end-time program.

Understanding the Rapture and God's program for the end times helps us see what God has planned for our world and our lives in the future. While there is certainly much that we don't know about the future, the truth of the Rapture and the events that follow it present a harmonized pattern of God's future plan and program for the church, the world, unbelievers, nations, and Satan.

The Rapture clarifies. It brings many things in God's Word and in the world around us into clearer focus and sharper perspective. And in these turbulent, chaotic times in which we live, focus and perspective are gifts of inestimable value.

May God be pleased to use the truths in this book to challenge, comfort, and clarify the issues of your life as you seek to live for Him.

APPENDIX

O ne of the important things that we need today in the body of Christ is to keep in touch with our past. Far too often we fail to remember the giants of the faith and our opportunities to continue to learn from them.

The information presented in this appendix was taken from a classic article from *Bibliotheca Sacra* by Dr. John Walvoord.[47] This article presents fifty arguments for pre-Tribulationism. It's the most comprehensive, concise article that I know of on this topic. The article is used by permission from Dr. Roy Zuck, the editor of *Bibliotheca Sacra*.

50 ARGUMENTS FOR PRETRIBULATIONISM

Dr. John F. Walvoord

I.   ***Historical Argument***

1. The early church believed in the imminency of the Lord's return, which is an essential doctrine of pre-Tribulationism.

2. The detailed development of pre-Tribulational truth during the past few centuries does not prove that the doctrine is new or novel. Its development is similar to that of other major doctrines in the history of the church.

II.   *Hermeneutics*

3. Pre-Tribulationism is the only view that allows a literal interpretation of all Old and New Testament passages on the Great Tribulation.

4. Only pre-Tribulationism distinguishes clearly between Israel and the church and their respective programs.

III.   *The Nature of the Tribulation*

5. Pre-Tribulationism maintains the Scriptural distinction between the Great Tribulation and tribulation in general, which precedes it.

6. The Great Tribulation is properly interpreted by pre-Tribulationists as a time of preparation for Israel's restoration (see Deut. 4:29–30; Jer. 30:4–11). It is not the purpose of the Tribulation to prepare the church for glory.

7. None of the Old Testament passages on the Tribulation mentions the church (see Deut. 4:29–30; Jer. 30:4–11; Dan. 9:24–27; 12:1–2).

8. None of the New Testament passages on the Tribulation mentions the church (see Matt. 24:15–31; 1 Thess. 1:9–10; 5:4–9; Rev. 4–19).

9. In contrast to mid-Tribulationism, the pre-Tribulational view provides an adequate explanation for the

beginning of the Great Tribulation in Revelation 6. Mid-Tribulationism is refuted by the plain teaching of Scripture that the Great Tribulation begins long before the seventh trumpet of Revelation 11.

10. The proper distinction is maintained between the prophetic trumpets of Scripture by pre-Tribulationism. There is no proper ground for the pivotal argument of mid-Tribulationism that the seventh trumpet of Revelation is the last trumpet in that there is no established connection between the seventh trumpet of Revelation 11, the last trumpet of 1 Corinthians 15:52, and the trumpet of Matthew 24:31. They are three distinct events.

11. The unity of Daniel's seventieth week is maintained by pre-Tribulationists. By contrast, mid-Tribulationism destroys the unity of Daniel's seventieth week and confuses Israel's program with that of the church.

IV.   The Nature of the Church

12. The translation of the church is never mentioned in any passage dealing with the second coming of Christ after the Tribulation.

13. The church is not appointed to wrath (see Rom. 5:9; 1 Thess. 1:9–10; 5:9). The church therefore cannot enter "the great day of their wrath" (Rev. 6:17).

14. The church will not be overtaken by the Day of the Lord (see 1 Thess. 5:1–9), which includes the Tribulation.

15. The possibility of a believer escaping the Tribulation is mentioned in Luke 21:36.

16. The church of Philadelphia was promised deliverance from the "hour of trial, that hour which is to come upon the whole world, to try them that dwell upon the earth" (Rev. 3:10).

17. It is characteristic of divine dealing to deliver believers before a divine judgment is inflicted upon the world as illustrated in the deliverance of Noah, Lot, Rahab, etc. (see 2 Pet. 2:6–9).

18. At the time of the translation of the church, all believers go to the Father's house in heaven and do not remain on the earth as taught by post–Tribulationists (see John 14:3).

19. Pre-Tribulationism does not divide the body of Christ at the Rapture on a works principle. The teaching of a partial Rapture is based on the false doctrine that the translation of the church is a reward for good works. It is rather a climactic aspect of salvation by grace.

20. The Scriptures clearly teach that all, not part, of the church will be raptured at the coming of Christ for the church (see 1 Cor. 15:51–52; 1 Thess. 4:17).

21. As opposed to a view of a partial Rapture, pre–Tribulationism is founded on the definite teaching of Scripture that the death of Christ frees from all condemnation.

22. The godly remnant of the Tribulation are depicted as Israelites, not as members of the church as maintained by the post-Tribulationists.

23. The pre-Tribulational view as opposed to post-Tribulationism does not confuse general terms like *elect* and *saints*, which apply to the saved of all ages with specific phrases like "the church" and those "in Christ," which refer to believers of this age only.

V.   *The Doctrine of Imminency*

24. The pre-Tribulational interpretation is the only view that teaches that the coming of Christ is actually imminent.

25. The exhortation to be comforted by the coming of the Lord (see 1 Thess. 4:18) is significant only in the pre-Tribulational view, and it is especially contradicted by post-Tribulationism.

26. The exhortation to look for "the glorious appearing" (Titus 2:13) loses its significance if the Tribulation must intervene first. Believers in that case should look for signs.

27. The exhortation to purify ourselves in view of the Lord's return has the most significance if His coming is imminent (see 1 John 3:2–3).

28. The church is uniformly exhorted to look for the coming of the Lord, while believers in the Tribulation are directed to look for signs.

VI.   The Work of the Holy Spirit

29. The Holy Spirit as the restrainer of evil cannot be taken out of the world unless the church, which the Spirit indwells, is translated at the same time. The Tribulation cannot begin until this restraint is lifted.

30. The Holy Spirit as the restrainer must be taken out of the world before "the lawless one," who dominates the Tribulation period, can be revealed (2 Thess. 2:6–8).

31. If the expression "except the falling away come first" is translated literally, "except the departure come first," it would plainly show the necessity of the Rapture taking place before the beginning of the Tribulation.

VII.   The Necessity of an Interval Between the Rapture and Second Coming

32. According to 2 Corinthians 5:10, all believers of this age must appear before the judgment seat of Christ in heaven, an event that is never mentioned in the detailed accounts connected with the second coming of Christ to earth.

33. If the twenty-four elders of Revelation 4:1–5:14 are representative of the church, as many expositors believe, it would necessitate the Rapture and reward of the church before the Tribulation.

34. The marriage of Christ and the church must be celebrated in heaven before the second coming to the earth for the wedding feast (see Rev. 19:7–10).

35. Tribulation saints are not translated at the second coming of Christ but carry on ordinary occupations such as farming and building houses and shall bear children (see Isa. 65:20–25). This would be impossible if all saints were translated at the second coming to the earth as post-Tribulationists teach.

36. The judgment of the Gentiles following the Second Coming (see Matt. 25:31–46) indicates that both saved and unsaved are still in the natural bodies, which would be impossible if the translation had taken place at the Second Coming.

37. If the translation took place in connection with the second coming to the earth, there would be no need of separating the sheep from the goats at a subsequent judgment, but the separation would have taken place in the very act of the translation of the believers before Christ actually came to the earth.

38. The judgment of Israel (see Ezek. 20:34–38) that occurs subsequent to the Second Coming indicates

the necessity of regathering Israel. The separation of the saved from the unsaved in this judgment obviously takes place sometime after the Second Coming and would be unnecessary if a translation of the saved had taken place previously.

VIII.   Contrasts Between the Rapture and the Second Coming

39. At the time of the Rapture the saints meet Christ in the air, while at the Second Coming Christ returns to the Mount of Olives to meet the saints on earth.

40. At the time of the Rapture the Mount of Olives is unchanged, while at the Second Coming it divides and a valley is formed to the east of Jerusalem (see Zecharia 14:4–5).

41. At the Rapture living saints are translated, while no saints are translated in connection with the second coming of Christ to the earth.

42. At the Rapture the saints go to heaven, while at the second coming to the earth the saints remain in the earth without translation.

43. At the time of the Rapture the world is unjudged and continues in sin, while at the Second Coming the world is judged and righteousness is established in the earth.

44. The translation of the church is pictured as a deliverance before the day of wrath, while the Second Coming is followed by the deliverance of those who have believed in Christ during the Tribulation.

45. The Rapture is described as imminent, while the Second Coming is preceded by definite signs.

46. The translation of living believers is truth revealed only in the New Testament, while the Second Coming, with its attendant events, is a prominent doctrine of both Testaments.

47. The Rapture concerns only the saved, while the Second Coming deals with both saved and unsaved.

48. At the Rapture Satan is not bound, while at the Second Coming Satan is bound and cast into the abyss.

49. No unfulfilled prophecy stands between the church and the Rapture, while many signs must be fulfilled before the Second Coming.

50. No passage dealing with the resurrection of saints at the Second Coming in either Testament ever mentions a translation of living saints at the same time.

A PROPOSED
CHRONOLOGY OF
THE END TIMES

In many of my books on end-time prophecy I like to include this outline at the end. I recognize that it's not easy trying to fit together all the pieces of the end times into a chronological sequence. This outline is my best attempt, at this time, to accomplish that task. I certainly wouldn't insist on the correctness of every detail in this outline, but my prayer is that it will help you get a better grasp of the overall flow of events in the end times.

I. Events in Heaven

A. **The Rapture of the Church** (see 1 Corinthians 15:51–58; 1 Thessalonians 4:13–18; Revelation 3:10)

B. **The Judgment Seat of Christ** (see Romans 14:10; 1 Corinthians 3:9–15; 4:1–5; 9:24–27; 2 Corinthians 5:10)

C. The Marriage of the Lamb (see 2 Corinthians 11:2; Revelation 19:6–8)

D. The Singing of Two Special Songs (see Revelation 4–5)

E. The Lamb Receiving the Seven-Sealed Scroll (see Revelation 5)

II. Events on Earth

A. Seven-Year Tribulation

1. Beginning of the Tribulation

a. Seven-year Tribulation begins when the Antichrist signs a covenant with Israel, bringing peace to Israel and Jerusalem (see Daniel 9:27; Ezekiel 38:8, 11).

b. The Jewish temple in Jerusalem is rebuilt (see Daniel 9:27; Revelation 11:1).

c. The reunited Roman empire emerges in a ten-nation confederation (see Daniel 2:40–44; 7:7; Revelation 17:12).

2. First half (three and a half years) of the Tribulation

a. The seven seal judgments are opened (see Revelation 6).

b. The 144,000 Jewish believers begin their great evangelistic ministry (see Revelation 7).

c. Gog and his allies invade Israel, while Israel is at peace under the covenant with Antichrist and are supernaturally decimated by God (see Daniel 11:40–45; Ezekiel 38–39). This will probably occur somewhere near the end of the three-and-a-half-year period. The destruction of these forces will create a major shift in the balance of power that will enable the Antichrist to begin his rise to world ascendancy.

3. The midpoint of the Tribulation

a. Antichrist breaks his covenant with Israel and invades the land (see Daniel 9:27; 11:40–41).

b. Antichrist begins to consolidate his empire by plundering Egypt, Sudan, and Libya, whose armies have just been destroyed by God in Israel (see Daniel 11:42–43; Ezekiel 38–39).

c. While in North Africa, Antichrist hears disturbing news of insurrection in Israel and immediately returns there to destroy and annihilate many (see Daniel 11:44).

d. Antichrist sets up the abomination of desolation in the rebuilt temple in Jerusalem (see Daniel 9:27; 11:45; Matthew 24:15; 2 Thessalonians 2:4; Revelation 13:5, 15–18).

e. Sometime during these events the Antichrist is violently killed, possibly as a result of a war or assassination (see Revelation 13:3, 12, 14; 17:8).

f. Satan is cast down from heaven and begins to make war with the woman, Israel (see Revelation 12:7–13). The chief means that he uses to persecute Israel is the two beasts in Revelation 13.

g. The faithful Jewish remnant flee to Petra in modern Jordan, where they are divinely protected for the remainder of the Tribulation (see Matthew 24:16–20; Revelation 12:15–17).

h. The Antichrist is miraculously raised from the dead to the awestruck amazement of the entire world (see Revelation 13:3).

i. After his resurrection from the dead, the Antichrist gains political control over the ten kings of the reunited Roman empire. Three of these kings will be killed by the Antichrist, and the other seven will submit (see Daniel 7:24; Revelation 17:12–13).

j. The two witnesses begin their three-and-a-half-year ministry (see Revelation 11:2–3).

k. Antichrist and the ten kings destroy the religious system of Babylon and set up their religious capital in the city (see Revelation 17:16–17).

4. *Last half (three and a half years) of the Tribulation*

a. Antichrist blasphemes God, and the false prophet performs great signs and wonders and promotes false worship of the Antichrist (see Revelation 13:5, 11–15).

b. The mark of the beast (666) is introduced and enforced by the false prophet (see Revelation 13:16–18).

c. Totally energized by Satan, the Antichrist dominates the world politically, religiously, and economically (see Revelation 13:4–5, 15–18).

d. The Trumpet Judgments are unleashed throughout the final half of the Tribulation (see Revelation 8–9).

e. Knowing that he has only a short time left, Satan intensifies his relentless, merciless persecution of the Jewish people and Gentile believers on earth (see Daniel 7:25; Revelation 12:12; 13:15; 20:4).

5. *The end of the Tribulation*

  a. The bowl judgments are poured out in rapid succession (see Revelation 16).
  b. The campaign of Armageddon begins (see Revelation 16:16).
  c. Commercial Babylon is destroyed (see Revelation 18).
  d. The two witnesses are killed by Antichrist and are resurrected by God three and a half days later (see Revelation 11:7–12).
  e. Christ returns to the Mount of Olives and slays the armies gathered against Him throughout the land, from Megiddo to Petra (see Revelation 19:11–16; Isaiah 34:1–6; 63:1–5).
  f. The birds gather to feed on the carnage (see Revelation 19:17–18).

B. After the Tribulation

1. *Interval or transition period of seventy-five days (see Daniel 12:12).*

  a. The Antichrist and the false prophet are cast in the lake of fire (see Revelation 19:20–21).
  b. The abomination of desolation is removed from the temple (see Daniel 12:11).
  c. Israel is regathered (see Matthew 24:31).

    d. Israel is judged (see Ezekiel 20:30–39; Matthew 25:1–30).

    e. Gentiles are judged (see Matthew 25:31–46).

    f. Satan is bound in the abyss (see Revelation 20:1–3).

    g. Old Testament and Tribulation saints are resurrected (see Daniel 12:1–3; Isaiah 26:19; Revelation 20:4).

2. *One-thousand-year reign of Christ on earth (see Revelation 20:4–6).*

3. *Satan's final revolt and defeat (see Revelation 20:7–10).*

4. *The Great White Throne Judgment of the lost (see Revelation 20:11–15).*

5. *The destruction of the present heavens and earth (see Matthew 24:35; 2 Peter 3:3–12; Revelation 21:1).*

6. *The creation of the new heavens and new earth (see Isaiah 65:17; 66:22; 2 Peter 3:13; Revelation 21:1).*

7. *Eternity (see Revelation 21:9–22:5).*

NOTES

1. *The Lamplighter*, Lion and Lamb Ministries (September-October 2000).
2. David J. Jefferson and Anne Underwood, "The Pop Prophets," *Newsweek*, 24 May 2004, 48.
3. Three factors indicate that Paul was in Thessalonica for more than three weeks: (1) During Paul's stay in Thessalonica, the believers in Philippi sent at least two financial gifts to Paul (Philippians 4:16). Since Thessalonica is about one hundred miles away, this points to a considerable lapse of time. (2) Paul was in Thessalonica long enough to pursue his secular trade (see 1 Thessalonians 2:9). (3) The fact that most of the members of the Thessalonian church were Gentiles indicates that after reasoning with the Jews for three weeks in the synagogue, Paul had some time of ministry among the Gentiles in Thessalonica.
4. D. Edmond Hiebert, *1 & 2 Thessalonians* (Chicago: Moody Press, 1992), 211–2.
5. The reference to the trumpet in conjunction with the Rapture has lead many to believe that the Rapture will occur in the fall, during the Jewish feast of trumpets or Rosh Hashanah. I reject this notion for two main reasons. First, it destroys imminency. If the Rapture must occur some year during the feast of trumpets, then every year after this day passes a person could know for another

year that the Rapture couldn't occur. Second, the Jewish feasts primarily concern God's program for the Jewish people, not the church. The feast of trumpets will be fulfilled, not by the church at the Rapture before the Tribulation, but at the end of the Tribulation, when the Jewish people are gathered from all over the world back to their land to live under the rule of their Messiah. At that time Matthew 24:31 will be fulfilled.

6. John F. Walvoord, *The Thessalonian Epistles* (Grand Rapids: Lamplighter Books, n.d.), 44.

7. John F. MacArthur, Jr., *1 Corinthians* (Chicago: Moody Press, 1984), 444.

8. Andy Stanley, *How Good Is Good Enough?* (Sisters, OR: Multnomah Publishers, 2003), 7–8.

9. A Greek English Lexicon of the New Testament, 80.

10. Hiebert, 215.

11. Many scholars have noted a connection between John 14:1–3 and 1 Thessalonians 4:13–18. Renald Showers cites several individuals such as J. H. Bernard, James Montgomery Boice, Arno C. Gaebelein, Arthur Pink, Rudolf Schnackenburg, F. F. Bruce, R. V. G. Tasker, and W. E. Vine in *Maranatha: Our Lord Come!* (Bellmawr, NJ: Friends of Israel, 1995), 162.

12. This chart was taken from J. B. Smith, *A Revelation of Jesus Christ: A Commentary on the Book of Revelation* (Scottdale, PA: Herald Press, 1961), 311–3.

13. Many others have pointed to Moses as one of the two witnesses. There are three main points in favor of identifying Moses as one of the two witnesses. First, like Moses, the two witnesses will turn the rivers to blood and bring other plagues on the earth (see Revelation 11:6). Second, on the Mount of Transfiguration, which pictured the second coming glory of Christ, Moses and Elijah appeared with Christ (see Matthew 17:1–11). Third, Moses was a prophet.

14. Some might also see John's transfer to heaven in Revelation 4:1 as a personal rapture. But since the word *harpazo* is not used there, I

have omitted it from the list of rapture events. Many pre-Tribbers believe that Revelation 4:1 describes the rapture of the church due to the parallels with 1 Thessalonians 4:13–18: a voice, a trumpet, and a call to come up. The timing of this event fits the pre-Tribulationist scheme nicely since Revelation 4:1 occurs right after the discussion of the churches and right before the beginning of the Tribulation. In spite of the attractiveness of this view to my position, I reject it for three reasons. First, John goes up for revelation, not glorification. Second, it appears that John's body stayed on earth and that he was transported by means of a vision. Third, Revelation 4:1 describes John, not the church, going up.

15. Gerald B. Stanton, *Kept from the Hour* (Miami Springs, FL: Schoettle Publishing Co., 1991), 166.

16. Warren Wiersbe, *Be Myself: Memoirs of a Bridgebuilder* (Wheaton, IL: Victor Books, 1994), 263–4.

17. John F. Walvoord, *The Return of the Lord* (Grand Rapids: Zondervan, 1955), 88. The quotation and the first six contrasts in the comparison above are taken from pp. 87–8 of Walvoord's *The Return*.

18. John F. MacArthur, *The Second Coming* (Wheaton: Crossway Books, 1999), 87.

19. In Revelation there are three series of seven judgments: the seals, trumpets, and bowls. This, of course, equals twenty-one. But since the seventh seal contains the seven trumpets and the seventh trumpet contains the seven bowls, the total number of specific judgments is actually nineteen rather than twenty-one.

20. Billy Graham, *World Aflame* (Old Tappan, NJ: Fleming H. Revell Company, 1965), 173.

21. J. F. Strombeck, 133.

22. Gleason L. Archer, *The Rapture: Pre* , 117–8.

23. Walvoord, *The Thessalonian Epistles*, 54.

24. Ibid., 73.

25. For a thorough, scholarly discussion of this issue and many other issues related to the timing of the Rapture, see Gleason L. Archer,

Jr., Paul D. Feinberg, et al, *The Rapture: Pre-, Mid-, or Post-Tribulational?* (Grand Rapids: Academie Books, 1984), 63–71.

26. Charles C. Ryrie, *Come Quickly, Lord Jesus* (Eugene, OR: Harvest House Publishers, 1996), 137–8.

27. Of course, the mid-Tribulationist view and the pre-Wrath view also allow for a time gap between the Rapture and the Second Coming. For the mid-Tribulationist view the interval is three and a half years, and for the pre-Wrath view it's about one and a half years. But the time gap of at least seven years for the pre-Tribulationst view is the best alternative.

28. Donald Grey Barnhouse, *Thessalonians: An Expositional Commentary* (Grand Rapids: Zondervan Publishing House, 1977), 99–100.

29. Thomas Ice, "Imminency and the Any Moment Rapture," *Pre-Trib Perspectives* (October 1999): 3.

30. Ibid., 22.

31. Renald Showers, *Maranatha Our Lord Come! A Definitive Study of the Rapture of the Church* (Bellmawr, NJ: The Friends of Israel Gospel Ministry, Inc., 1995), 127–8.

32. Ibid., 127.

33. Ice, 4.

34. Mayhue, 218–9.

35. Paul J. Alexander, *The Byzantine Apocalyptic Tradition* (Berkeley: University of California Press, 1985), 136.

36. Timothy J. Demy and Thomas D. Ice, "The Rapture and Pseudo-Ephraem: An Early Medieval Citation," *Bibliotheca Sacra* 152 (July–September 1995): 12.

37. Francis Gumerlock, "A Rapture Citation in the Fourteenth Century," *Bibliotheca Sacra* 159 (July-September 2002): 354–5.

38. Ibid., 356–9.

39. Ibid., 361.

40. Morgan Edwards, *Two Academical Exercises on Subjects Bearing the following Titles; Millennium, Last-Novelties* (Philadelphia: Self-published, 1788), 7.

41. Ibid.

42. Thomas Ice and Timothy Demy, *The Truth About the Tribulation* (Eugene, OR: Harvest House Publishers, 1996), 46.

43. MacArthur, *The Second Coming*, 88.

44. Tim LaHaye, *The Rapture: Who Will Face the Tribulation?* (Eugene, OR: Harvest House Publishers, 2002), 71–2.

45. The URL for this site is http://www.bible.ca/pre-date-setters.htm.

46. Charles Dyer, *World News and Bible Prophecy* (Wheaton: Tyndale House Publishers, 1995), 270.

47. John F. Walvoord, "Conclusion: 50 Arguments for Pretribulationism," *Bibliotheca Sacra* (July 1957): 193–9.

Also from **Mark Hitchcock**

55 Answers to Questions About Life After Death
1-59052-436-5 • $12.99

The Truth Behind Left Behind
1-59052-366-0 • $12.99